THE KITCHEN WITCH

THE KITCHEN WITCH

SEASONAL RECIPES, LOTIONS, AND POTIONS FOR

EVERY PAGAN FESTIVAL

SORAYA

Interlink Books

An imprint of Interlink Publishing Group, Inc.
Northampton, Massachusetts

First published in 2021 by
INTERLINK BOOKS
An imprint of Interlink Publishing Group, Inc.
46 Crosby Street
Northampton, Massachusetts 01060
www.interlinkbooks.com

Text © Soraya, 2021
Design © Interlink Publishing Group, Inc. 2021
Illustrations © Martin Conway, 2021

Library of Congress Cataloging-in-Publication Data available
ISBN 978-1-62371-861-9

Publisher: Michel Moushabeck
Editors: Jennifer Staltare and Leyla Moushabeck
Designer: Harrison Williams
Proofreader: Jane Bugaeva

For our complete catalog visit our website at www.interlinkbooks.com or e-mail: sales@interlinkbooks.com

Printed and bound in the USA

10 9 8 7 6 5 4 3 2 1

CONTENTS

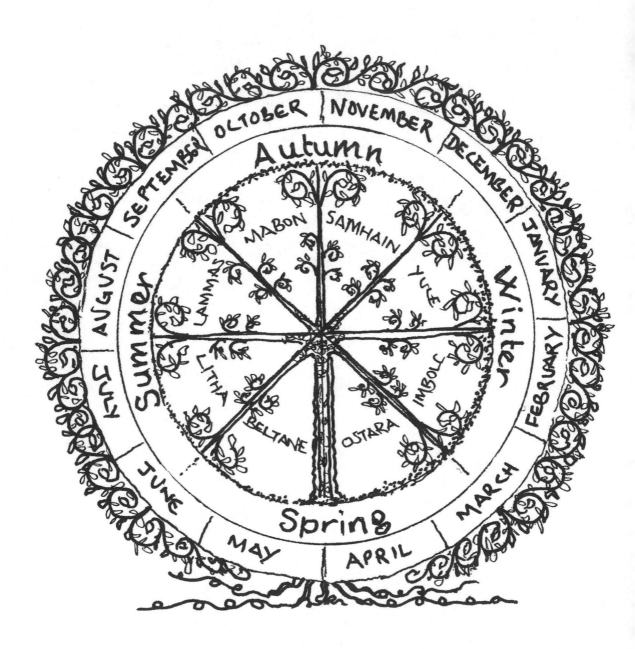

THE KITCHEN GODDESS

For me, cooking is a magickal experience. I feel most "witchy" when I am cooking, combining all my fresh Goddess-given ingredients, and concocting pure magick.

It is nothing like that clichéd image of the witch hunched over her bubbling cauldron—although I do have a cauldron!—but a meal prepared with love can be as potent as any potion.

I love cooking for people. It is a great way to show how much you care about them. If a meal is made with love then you are passing that energy on to your friends and loved ones. And if your entertaining is well-intentioned; you have taken care to make your surroundings welcoming, comfortable, and homey; and you, yourself are full of fun and positive energy, your dinner party will be a success, even if your soufflés flop and your custard splits.

If the kitchen witch has her heart in the home—and her kitchen is inevitably the heart of that home—she also often has her head in a book. Her cookbook is a culinary book of shadows that will be priceless to her, containing the knowledge of generations. Her cousin the hedge witch has much to add to this, with knowledge of the fruits of the hedgerow and the field. Wild plants, herbs, and foraged food are all goddess-given and there for the taking.

You do not have to be Wiccan to enjoy this book but if you are, here at your disposal are the means to celebrate all the Wiccan festivals with seasonal foods and magickal herbs and spices for all the rituals of the pagan year. I have also drawn on my Arab and Scottish roots for inspiration for some dishes.

WICCA AND ITS FESTIVALS

Wicca is a pagan, Goddess-based faith or belief system in which we recognize and acknowledge a supreme being—a being that is in the life-giving air that we breath, in the fire that warms us, in the water that washes us clean and sustains us, and in the earth that carries our weight. A pagan or Wiccan is someone who recognizes that this supreme being is made up of masculine and feminine elements—a god and goddess combined—Father God who reigns above us and Mother Earth beneath our feet. We believe in observing the laws and signs of nature, in life after death, in the goddess-given gifts of healing, and in the power of word, deed, and action—magick.

The word "witch" comes from the words "wise" or "wisdom"; originally witches or Wiccans were called "the wise ones." They are also healers who study natural remedies and the influences of the cycles of the moon and the planets. Witches seek to harm no one, knowing that the energy they send out comes back threefold.

Being a Wiccan or a witch is not just about magick and spells. Being a witch is about *being*—being at one with nature and all that surrounds us.

In pagan tradition, the four elements—air, fire, water, and earth—correspond in turn to the four points of the compass: air to the east, fire to the south, water to the west, and earth to the north. The face of the compass is round reminding us again of the cycles of birth, life, death, and rebirth. Wiccans also work within the cycles of the sun and the moon and the changing seasons, which are known in pagan terms as "the wheel of the year." We celebrate the wheel of the year with four great sabbats, or festivals, and four lesser sabbats. The eight festivals are:

SAMHAIN

A greater sabbat that is celebrated on October 31st.

YULE (THE WINTER SOLSTICE)

A lesser sabbat that is celebrated on December 21st.

IMBOLC

A greater sabbat that is celebrated on February 2nd.

OSTARA (THE SPRING EQUINOX)

A lesser sabbat that is celebrated on March 20th.

BELTANE

A greater sabbat that is celebrated on May 1st.

LITHA (THE SUMMER SOLSTICE)

A lesser sabbat that is celebrated on June 21st.

LAMMAS (LUGHNASADH)

A greater sabbat that is celebrated on August 1st.

MABON (THE AUTUMN EQUINOX)

A lesser sabbat that is celebrated on September 22nd.

During these Wiccan festivals we recognize and celebrate the birth, life, death, and rebirth of the God and Goddess and their union. As with any festival, the celebrations involve sharing food with loved ones or friends, just as you would at many other holiday celebrations.

Wiccans work their craft on an empty stomach, whether they are working alone as a solo or solitary or with friends in a coven. But afterwards, it is customary to enjoy something nice to eat that is also relevant to the season. Wiccans are at one with nature and have an understanding of the magickal powers of plants, herbs, spices, and other foods, so this knowledge is ofen applied in the preparation of our menus. Our celebration foods complement any spell work that we may be casting, and sharing that food with others is an added blessing that empowers the strength of the spell.

The chapters that follow contain recipes for each of the eight pagan sabbats. These are not prescriptive menus for a whole banquet but ideas to inspire you.

In the first chapter you will find basic recipes that are suitable for all of the Wiccan festivals using a variety of foods usually found in your kitchen, as well as a list of herbs and essential oils that you can use for spell or circle work. These basic recipes can all be adapted to suit your particular requirements. Use these guides to help you choose which herbs to use with which foods and rituals. Do not make a meal incdible by forcing flavors together—that would defeat the purpose of creating a truly magickal meal in taste and intention!

The chapters that follow contain over 200 recipes to inspire you to cook for the eight pagan sabbats. Some are recipes my mom taught me, though she would never tell me or my sisters the full list of ingredients, always keeping a secret something to herself. This is typical witch behavior—though she never admitted to being a witch or to keeping secrets! Enjoy these recipes, experiment with them, and improvise with your own ingredients. If you are not pagan, use this book to help give you an awareness of the cycle of life and the seasons. It is not just witches who can create magickal feasts!

FRESH OR PRE-MADE?

When I was a child, I can remember going shopping with my mom and I don't believe I ever saw her buy a pre-cooked, pre-packaged meal. There were never any store-bought sauces or cake mixes in her pantry. Everything we ate was cooked from scratch. I am sure that this was also the case with my friends' families. The result of this is that my generation learned to cook healthy and hearty meals from any kind of natural ingredients. Today when I go grocery shopping there are rows and rows of mixes and pre-packaged, pre-cooked meals.

The result all of this highly processed, pre-cooked food is that many young folk cannot cook and do not know or do not care what they are eating. In fact, I recall my daughter telling me that one of her teenage friends didn't know that chips could be made from potatoes!

When your children eat a lot of pre-packaged food they have no idea what good, fresh food tastes like. Their palate can be dulled by high-fat, sugary, high-salt foods and the chemicals used to preserve them, so that when they are presented with nutritious, tasty food made from fresh ingredients they often turn their noses up at it!

Worse than that, when eating processed pre-made meals, you are eating food that was prepared by strangers under unknown conditions. You have no real idea what you are eating or where the ingredients came from and you have no way of knowing in what kind of environment the food was prepared. We get our energy from the air that we breathe, the company that we keep, and especially the food that we eat. Suppose someone is dissatisfied with their working conditions or pay—what kind of mood are they in when preparing or packaging your food? If someone is angry and resentful when they are cooking, this is the energy that they bring to the food, and this is the energy that the consumer takes into their bodies.

I am just like everyone else—there are some days when I just can't be bothered to cook. So on the days that I do cook I tend to make much more than I need and freeze the rest for my lazy or too-busy days. I avoid store-bought meals and processed foods with few exceptions, and I never eat food that has been microwaved. I use fresh and organic ingredients whenever I can. I don't even use teabags—or, as I call them, bags of tea dust! I much prefer infusions of herbs or tea leaves. You can read tea leaves; you cannot read a tea bag—or, at least, I have never tried!

EATING OUT

I never eat in restaurants unless I am certain that the food is good and fresh and that the staff are well treated and friendly. This, I must admit, can be difficult to accomplish, but once I find a suitable place, I seldom go anywhere else. I trust my instincts as well and have walked out of restaurants because I felt uncomfortable with the energy or atmosphere. Whenever I go into a new place to eat I have several guidelines that I follow:

a)   Does the outside look clean, bright, and welcoming? If the operators care about the outside presentation of their restaurant, chances are they will care about the inside too.

b)   Is it busy? If so, chances are it has a good reputation and the food will be fresher.

c)   Are the table and chairs clean? I hate to touch the back of a chair and find that it is grubby.

d)   I always ask if the food is cooked on the premises and if they use a microwave to reheat it.

GETTING BACK TO THE LAND

I remember when going food shopping was an energizing community experience. We met friends and neighbors as we waited in line to be served. We chatted about each other's lives and families. We admired the seasonal produce that had just been delivered. Our grocery store was independently owned and our vegetables were fresh and grown locally. Down the road we would go to the butcher's shop. He knew everyone by name and would ask after family members. The meat we bought was fresh and came from a farm not far away. Next we would go to the fishmonger's to buy fish that was freshly caught and delivered that morning from nearby fishing towns. Everyone knew everyone else. The community was supported and the land was protected.

Today, we frequently jump in the car and head to the nearest or biggest superstore, where we fill a cart with processed foods that someone else has prepared. Chances are we will not see anyone that we know and we will only talk to the checkout operator. We can find everything under one roof—oh so convenient, but at what price? Our health suffers and so too does the land. Local farmers who grow their crops free of chemicals and with respect for the land are rapidly being squeezed out of business by large-scale farms who can supply superstores with more products for less money—all to satisfy the greed of large corporations and the laziness of consumers. We face climate change and an increase in livestock diseases, and much of our produce is saturated with chemicals and trucked in.

You might ask yourself what all this has to do with being a witch. The answer is, everything! As Wiccans, we believe that we are sustained by and at one with nature; the earth's energy impacts everything we do. For the sake of the land and ourselves, is time for us to return to the land and live in harmony with nature.

I urge you to think about how you live and how you get your energy. Think about what you eat and where it came from. Avoid processed foods as much as possible and start preparing delicious meals, from the land to your table. Whenever you can, support farmers' markets and grow your own herbs and vegetables. Be mindful of the seasons and the elements, and your state of mind when you cook. Get this part right and your spells will take care of themselves. Soon everything that you touch will be magickal and you will know when the Goddess is walking with you, guiding you, and changing your life. Now that is what I call magick!

CHAPTER ONE

TO BEGIN ...

Here you will find a guide to herbs, spices, and edible flowers, and their magickal uses. Additionally, there are certain cooking methods and recipes that crop up in each season in many different variations, and I thought it best to put them here. You can add your own touch to these basic recipes, adding the herbs and spices that will personalize your spells and cooking, and that are seasonally appropriate for the pagan festivals throughout the year.

HERBS AND SPICES GUIDE

The list that follows provides a summary of herbs to use in meals following a ritual. There are also flowers, plants, and barks that are not advised for eating but could decorate or scent your altar or dining room. Alternatively, you can use the essential or aromatic oils of any of these plants in your ritual work. I have also included a list of edible flowers, but it is safest to consult a specialist book on this subject.

Love:
In your food: sorrel • vanilla • cinnamon • coriander • cilantro
In the dining room: rose • tansy • gardenia • mimosa

Money:
In your food: basil • dill • cinnamon • ginger • spearmint • allspice • chamomile
In the dining room: honeysuckle

Luck
In your food: allspice • comfrey • nutmeg • heather
In the dining room: fern • clover • shamrock

Insight:
In your food: orange • lemongrass • marjoram
In the dining room: sage • lily • cypress • hibiscus

Protection
In your food: angelica • basil

• bay • cinnamon • cloves • coriander • cilantro• dill • garlic • mint • peppermint • pepper • marjoram
In the dining room: cedarwood • frankincense • lilac

Success
In your food: bay • chamomile • lovage • rosemary • saffron • marjoram
In the dining room: sweet pea • marigold • bergamot

Wisdom
In your food: bay • chamomile • dill • parsley • sage • marjoram • borage • chervil • cumin • sage • thyme
In the dining room: violet

Travel
In your food: caraway • dill • fennel • marjoram • mustard • parsley
In the dining room: lavender

Courage
In your food: pepper • basil • chives • horseradish • nettle • pepper
In the dining room: honeysuckle

Peace
In your food: marjoram • mint • clary sage • sage • lemon balm
In the dining room: carnation • jasmine • myrrh • wisteria

Happiness
In your food: cinnamon • feverfew • mint
In the dining room: apple blossom • frankincense

Fertility
In your food: cinnamon • mint • coriander

Health
In your food: allspice • cinnamon • angelica • coriander • cilantro poppyseed • chamomile

CULINARY AND MAGICKAL USES OF HERBS AND SPICES

If an herb is sweet and subtle, I will use it for love and romance. I will also be guided by the color of the blossom. For example, if the blossom is pink then I will use it for love, and if yellow or gold for finances and so on.

Then I think about the taste of the herb or spice. If strong, hot, and fiery, I would use it for protection and banishing, but I would also use hot spices as a booster to combine with something that I wanted to achieve in a hurry.

I suggest that you experiment and use your instincts, since they will guide you better than any book. Magick should be the most natural process, so let it flow naturally. When you are using plants to enhance your rituals, here are a few things to think about.

- the conditions they like to grow in—sunny, shady, wet, or dry
- what color the flowers are—the color can help to boost your work
- the type of bloom—tall or short, single or in clusters

All these things can help you to choose the right ingredient. Borage, for example (in Edible Flowers, page 21), is bright blue but keeps its head low, pointing at the earth, and only when you turn the flower over do you see its true magnificence. Based on the fact that the flower head looks downwards, I use borage for confidentiality, humility, and grounding. Because it looks downwards to the earth and so is aware of all that is happening; insight and awareness would be another good use.

Allspice is used in pickling, cakes, and pies. Use at Yule in cooking, baking, or in making your own atomizers. **Magickal uses**: wealth and healing.

Angelica (has edible flowers) can be added to cakes and cookies and works well with fish and salads. **Magickal uses**: protection.

Asafetida has an unpleasant smell but is transformed when cooked in oil to be oniony. **Magickal uses**: protection, banishing, dispels problems.

Basil (has edible flowers) goes well with tomato dishes. **Magickal uses**: love, relationships, wealth, healing, and protection spells.

Its strong smell makes it useful for dispelling negativity.

Bouquet garni (page 23) is a collection of herbs, commonly a bay leaf, parsley, and thyme, tied together and used in soups, stews, and casseroles. **Magickal uses**: boost spells in the manner of a bind rune (a symbol that combines two or more runic letters to create combined runic energies).

Caraway seeds are used in cakes, stir-fries, meat dishes, breads, and cheeses. **Magickal uses**: best used for loyalty and protection.

Cardamom, green has a lovely aroma and is delicious in rice puddings and other desserts. **Magickal uses:** love, passion, and matters of the heart.

Cardamom, black is best used in meat dishes. **Magickal uses**: healing, protection, and banishing.

Celery seeds are great in soups, breads, sauces, and casseroles. **Magickal uses**: improving concentration and increasing psychic awareness as well as building confidence.

Chili (all varieties) can be used for salads and main courses. **Magickal uses**: protection, passion, and as a booster to combine with other spell ingredients.

Chives (has edible flowers) are good in salads, egg mayonnaise, and with potatoes. **Magickal uses**: protection, healing, and stability.

Cinnamon great in sweet and savory foods—adds a flavorful but mild heat. **Magickal uses**: spiritual awareness, healing, protection, passion, and financial gain. Can boost other spices.

Cloves are used with ham, mulled wines, rice, and meats. **Magickal uses**: attracts wealth, banishes negative energy, and boosts other spells.

Cilantro (the leaf) is great in curries, sweet salads, spicy stews, carrot soup, or sweet chili dipping sauces. The seed **(coriander)** has a nutmeg-like taste and is great in spicy meat stews. **Magickal uses**: healing. The leaf is useful in banishing spells.

Cumin is used in a variety of curry and spicy dishes. **Magickal uses**: protection, loyalty, and love.

Dill is used with fish, fish cakes, and breads **Magickal uses**: protection and increasing wealth.

Fennel (has edible flowers) is good in bread and with pork and fish dishes. **Magickal uses**: love and protection.

Garlic (has edible flowers) is a versatile flavoring for savory dishess. Wild garlic (found in May) has edible stems and roots too. **Magickal uses**: protection, healing, and passion. (It should be noted that garlic essential oil, though a useful bactericide, is very, very pungent.)

Ginger has a lovely, aromatic heat to it that is good in both sweet and savory dishes. **Magickal uses:** passion, empowerment, courage, and boosting other ingredients.

Juniper berries complement meat, game, and pork and can be used to enhance drinks. **Magickal uses:** protection, healing, and love.

Lavender (has edible flowers) has wide and varied uses. Use to flavor (or scent) jams, jellies, cakes, cookies, and puddings. **Magickal uses:** love, healing, and protection.

Lemongrass is lovely with fish and can be used to flavor stocks and spicy soups. **Magickal uses:** romance, friendship, passion, and protection.

Marjoram (has edible flowers) can be used in all savory foods. **Magickal uses:** love, protection, and joy.

Mint (has edible flowers) is used in drinks, with potatoes, tomatoes, and meat dishes. **Magickal uses:** healing and protection and to boost other ingredients in spell work.

Mustard powder can be mixed with water or oil to make your own mustard. Add a pinch to cheese sauce. Rub it onto red meat before cooking. **Magickal uses:** protection and passion and to boost other ingredients in spell work.

Mustard seeds can be added to sauces or mashed potatoes. **Magickal uses:** protection, passion, and to boost other ingredients in spell work.

Nutmeg can be used in white sauce or added to mashed potatoes, fried mushrooms, soups, cakes, and a variety of other dishes. **Magickal uses:** health, wealth, good fortune, and for boosting other herbs or spices in ritual or spell work.

Oregano (has edible flowers) works really well in tomato dishes. **Magickal uses:** love, wealth, healing, relationships, and protection.

Paprika is a very mild pepper and is more often used for its color than its heat. For more flavor use smoked paprika. **Magickal uses:** passion, protection, and a mild boost to other spell ingredients.

Parsley is great in most savory foods. It can be chewed after eating garlic to remove the smell. **Magickal uses:** passion and protection.

Pepper (peppercorn) comes in several colors. Add pink to a creamy sauce for steak, green in marinades, and black in almost all savory foods (and it also complements strawberries). **Magickal uses:** works well as a booster for other ingredients in spells.

Use pink peppercorns for love and passion, green for healing, and black for everything else.

Poppyseeds are great with bread and sprinkled on pastry. **Magickal uses**: love, fertility, peace, and wealth.

Rosemary (has edible flowers) works well with pork, ham, lamb, and potatoes. It is very adaptable and can also be used in sweet dishes such as cakes, cookies, and preserves. **Magickal uses**: protection, passion, love, clarity, and healing.

Saffron is very expensive. It is added to rice and cake dishes for its color and delicate flavor. **Magickal uses**: save it for really special or extremely important situations and use for healing or depression.

Sage (has edible flowers) is lovely in soups and stews as well as in chicken and pork dishes. **Magickal uses**: protection, healing, wealth, and wisdom.

Sesame seeds are lovely in breads and pastry and in salads and stir-fries. **Magickal uses**: wealth and passion.

Sorrel has a sharp taste and is best used to garnish. **Magickal uses**: healing and love.

Tarragon has a mild but unique flavor that works well with chicken and fish dishes **Magickal uses**: gentle love, friendship, faith, healing, and resolving sensitive issues.

Thyme (has edible flowers) can be used to garnish soups, salads, breads, and savory pastries. **Magickal uses**: healing, wisdom, and courage.

Turmeric has a strong yellow color and for that reason it is often used as a substitute for saffron, but it can be bitter if you use too much. It works well with spicy dishes. **Magickal uses**: protection, banishing, and boosting other ingredients for spell work.

EDIBLE FLOWERS

I have included those flowers that I like to use. I only garnish foods with plants that I have grown from seed so I know what I'm eating is not a variant or hybrid of something. Do not use store-bought flowers, since there is little way of knowing if they have been treated with chemicals. Be wary when foraging for flowers because they may be contaminated with fumes from passing vehicles (among other things) or weedkillers. Only eat the petals because some pistils and stamens can be poisonous.

There are numerous specialist books on edible flowers and foraging that you should also consult. Do not put anything on the plate that cannot be eaten, and if you are unsure what it is, do not eat it!

Bergamot flowers can be used with fruits and salads. **Magickal uses**: wealth, clarity, and success.

Borage flowers have a beautiful blue color and a lovely star shape. Borage can be used in drinks, jellies, and salads. **Magickal uses**: confidentiality, humility, grounding, success, awareness, and drawing support from friends or colleagues.

Calendula or **pot marigold** can be used in soups, breads, cakes, and drinks. It is a healing plant. Pot Marigold Syrup (page 251) is wonderful for uplifting your spirit and easing sore throats. **Magickal uses**: healing.

Carnation petals make a lovely cake decoration and can be added to drinks. **Magickal uses**: protection and healing.

Chamomile flowers have a sweet taste and can be added to teas, juices, and salads. **Magickal uses**: wealth, peace, and protection.

Chervil flowers lose their flavor quickly so add them to salads or soups just before serving. **Magickal uses**: Protection, healing, and stability.

Chrysanthemums have a tangy taste and the petals can be used in salads. **Magickal uses**: protection.

Clover has a sweet liquorice taste and can be used in teas and salads. Dry and store red clover and use it in tea. **Magickal uses**: be guided by the color of the blossom and use for love, protection, or wealth and as a booster with other ingredients.

Cornflower comes in a wide variety of colors and makes a beautiful garnish. **Magickal uses**: be guided by the color of the blossom and use to suit the ritual or spell that you are working on.

Dandelion leaves can be made into a tea or eaten as salad leaves; the flowers can be made into wine; and the root can be used as a coffee substitute. **Magickal uses**: traditionally the seed heads can be blown to predict the outcome of events.

Elderflowers are beautiful as a garnish and delicious made into a wine, syrup, tea, or cordial (page 169). In pagan tradition, elder is a very magickal tree. **Magickal properties**: treats colds, allergies, and fevers; soothes stomach upsets, minor burns, and scratches; and aids sleep. In ritual magick, it is used for protection, fertility, or money worries.

Garlic flowers (white or pink) are lovely in salads. **Magickal uses**: protection, healing, and stability.

Lilac works well in salads (break off a few of the tiny flowers and scatter over your salad dish). You can make wine with the blossoms too. **Magickal uses**: protection.

Nasturtium petals can be used to garnish soups, salads, and cakes. **Magickal uses**: wealth, passion, and love.

Pansy petals can be used to garnish soups, salads, and cakes. **Magickal uses**: passion and love.

Rose petals can be used for juices, jellies, cake decoration, and summer teas. **Magickal uses**: be guided by the color of the blossom and use for protection, prediction, or love.

Sunflower petals can be used to garnish soups and savory or sweet dishes. **Magickal uses**: for growth and the expansion of any spell. It can also be used to banish negativity.

FLOWERS TO AVOID

Avoid anything you are unsure of eating. Among the flowers to avoid eating—and there are many—are azalea, crocus, daffodil, foxglove, lily of the valley, oleander, poinsettia, rhododendron, and wisteria.

A MAGICKAL BAG

To flavor soups, sauces, and stocks, you can gather together sprigs of this, stalks of that, and aromatic seeds and spices and tie them all up with a clean piece of cheesecloth and some string—a *bouquet garni*. Combine your cooking knowledge with your spellwork so the herbs complement the food and are also relevant to your ritual.

Dedicate the little bag of magick with a verse such as this:

> *This food is the blessing of the Gods.*
> *I remember those who have none.*
> *I am open and ready to receive that which is still to come.*
> *This little bag I dedicate,*
> *Filled with love and never hate. So mote it be.*

The mixture below will work well in most stocks to create good flavor. Try to keep a balance or some flavors may dominate. Try to remember that even if you do not like the taste of some things on their own (celery maybe!), they may be necessary as a flavor enhancer. You can use fresh or dried herbs:

> 1 bay leaf
> 1 sprig thyme
> 3 large sprigs parsley (including stalks)
> 4-inch (10 cm) celery stick (including leaves)
> Two 4-inch (10 cm) leeks
> 6 black peppercorns

Place all of the ingredients on a clean piece of cheesecloth and tie into a parcel using a clean piece of kitchen string. Use to flavor stocks and soups. Remove and discard before serving.

STOCK

You can make soup with water, but using stock will give it a fuller flavor. Now here is where cooking is similar to what might be done in a fictional witch's cauldron—though just for the record, I have never made stock from eye of newt or tongue of frog!

The following recipes are just guidelines. Once you know the theory you can adjust the flavors to make delicious stock out of pretty much any bones, meat, and vegetables you have on hand. Always save the carcass from roast chicken and the bones from roast meats. The bones can be raw but I think roasted bones make for a tastier stock (see page 26).

You need a lot of water since a lot of it evaporates. How much salt to add is a personal choice but I find 1 teaspoon per 4¼ cups (1 liter) of water is about right. If in doubt, wait until the end to add salt. If you are making stock from a ham hock there is probably no need to add extra salt, since ham can be very salty. Simmer for several hours without letting it boil. Boiling makes the stock cloudy.

Once the stock is made, you will need to chill it right away. It is very nutritious and therefore bacteria like to feast on it too, so keep it very cold; never let it sit at room temperature. Cool it down as quickly as possible before refrigerating or freezing it until needed. Never put hot stock straight in your refrigerator because it will reduce the temperature of everything else. Stock will keep for three days in the refrigerator or three months in the freezer.

BASIC BONE STOCK
Serves 4 to 6

> 2–3 lb (1–1.5 kg) raw or cooked bones
> Approx. 14½ cups (3.5 liters) water
> Salt (approximately 1 teaspoon per 4¼ cups/1 liter water)
> 2 celery sticks, cut into chunks
> 1 carrot, cut into chunks
> 1 onion, cut into chunks

Put the bones into a large stockpot and pour in enough water to generously cover them. Add the salt, bring to a boil, and then turn down the heat and simmer for 2–4 hours, depending on how flavorful you like your stock. Add more water as neccesary as the liquid evaporates. About 1 hour before the end of the cooking time, add the vegetables. Strain the liquid into a large bowl and discard the solids. Chill the stock in a basin of cold water until it is cool to the touch, then refrigerate or freeze until needed.

MEAT STOCK

Serves 4 to 6

2 onions, coarsely chopped

2 tablespoons (25 g) butter

1 lb 2 oz (500 g) leg of lamb or beef, or ham hock

1 small meat bone (that will easily fit in your pot)

14½ cups (3.5 liters) water

1 leek, coarsely chopped

2 celery sticks, coarsely chopped

1 carrot, coarsely chopped

1 *bouquet garni* (A Magickal Bag, page 23)

3½ teaspoons salt, or to taste (less if using ham)

Freshly ground black pepper

Melt the butter in large stockpot over medium-high heat and sauté the onions until brown. Add the meat, bone, and water to the pot and very slowly bring to a boil. Once boiling, skim the surface of any impurities, then turn the heat to low and simmer for 4 hours. Add the rest of the vegetables, *bouquet garni*, and salt and pepper to taste and simmer for a further 1 hour. Strain into a bowl, reserving some of the meat to use in soup if you wish. Chill the bowl of stock in a basin of cold water until it is cool, then refrigerate or freeze until needed. Skim any fat from the stock's surface before use. (Do not waste the fat; you can melt it over nuts and raisins to give to the birds in the form of a cake.)

CHICKEN STOCK

Serves 4 to 6

1 chicken carcass (leftover from a roast)

1 carrot, coarsely chopped

1 onion, coarsely chopped

1 celery stick, coarsely chopped

1 *bouquet garni* (A Magickal Bag, page 23)

12½ cups (3 liters) water

3 teaspoons salt, or to taste

Place all the ingredients in a stockpot. Bring to a boil, lower the heat, and simmer for 1–1½ hours. Strain, cool, then refrigerate or freeze until needed. Skim the fat from the surface before using.

FISH STOCK

Serves 4 to 6

Fish stock does not take hours to make, and that is the beauty of it. Just 30 minutes and you are done. You are making something delicious from stuff that will otherwise just get thrown away. Now that is what I call magick! Use this stock in dishes like seafood risotto or fish soup.

Fish heads, bones, and trimmings, shrimp tails, lobster shells
(anything like that, but never add gills or guts!)
4½ cups (1.1 liters) water, or more if needed
1 cup (240 ml) dry white wine, or more if needed
1 celery stick, coarsely chopped
1 clove garlic, crushed
1 onion, coarsely chopped
1 *bouquet garni* (A Magickal Bag, page 23; one including
sage, dill, and thyme works well)
6 black peppercorns
1 teaspoon salt

Put the fish bits in a large stockpot and add the water and white wine, making sure the ingredients are generously covered. Bring to a boil, skimming the surface to remove any impurities. Add the vegetables, *bouquet garni*, peppercorns, salt, and more water and wine to cover the ingredients, if needed. Lower the heat and simmer for 30 minutes. Remove from the heat and strain the stock into a bowl or container very carefully (you do not want any bones in your stock). Use immediately, or chill in a basin of cold water until it is cool, then refrigerate or freeze until needed. It will keep for up to three days in the refrigerator or two months in the freezer.

SHORTCRUST PASTRY *Makes enough to line a 6- to 8-inch (15-20 cm) pie pan*

Don't be scared of making pastry; it is really easy to do. Three tips for shortcrust: don't overwork it, keep all the ingredients (and your hands) cool, and let it rest in the fridge before you use it. You can use a food processor but take care not to mix for too long. For basic shortcrust, whatever amount of flour you use, use half that amount in fat (e.g., for 2 cups/240 g of flour, use 1 cup/225 g of butter). Some pastries have a bit more fat to yield a crumblier texture, but be aware that crumbly pastry is not so good for wetter pie fillings, since it can get soggy.

For sweet recipes, add 2 tablespoons sugar to the ingredients below. For a herb pastry, simply roll your finished dough over chopped herbs, fold once, then roll, fold twice, and roll again.

> 2¼ cups (250 g) self-rising flour
> A pinch of salt
> 9 tablespoons (125 g) butter
> 1–2 teaspoons water or milk

Put the flour, salt, butter, and sugar (if using) into a large bowl and rub together lightly and quickly using your fingers until it resembles fine breadcrumbs. Make a well in the center of the mixture and gradually add the water or milk, one teaspoon at a time. Using a knife, mix the dough until it leaves the sides of your bowl and is firm and not wet. (Always cut and stir pastry with a knife until it pulls together—never hands because warm hands melt the butter and spoils the results.) Cover the bowl and let it rest in the refrigerator for at least 30 minutes before using (or longer, it won't hurt).

Refer to individual recipes for cooking times and temperatures, but the general rule is to cook pastry at a high temperature for a short time, or "blind bake" it before adding fillings. This means baking a pastry shell with no filling in it at 400°F (200°C) for 10–12 minutes before filling it.

ROUGH PUFF PASTRY   *Makes enough to line a 6-inch (15 cm) pie pan*

1⅔ cups (200 g) all-purpose flour, plus extra for dusting
1 teaspoon salt
6 oz (150 g) butter, cut into cubes
A few drops lemon juice
½ cup (125 ml) cold water

In a mixing bowl, combine the flour and salt together. Using your fingers, rub the butter into the flour until it resembles breadcrumbs. Add the lemon juice and water, transfer to a mixer if you have one, and mix or knead to make an elastic dough.

Turn the dough out onto a floured work surface and roll it into an oblong strip. Dust with more flour, then fold the dough into three sections. Seal the edges using your fingers and give it a quarter turn. Roll out the dough again into an oblong strip, fold into three, seal the edges, and give it a quarter turn. Repeat this process four more times. Wrap the dough in plastic wrap and leave it to rest in the refrigerator for at least 30 minutes before using.

BREAD

Makes three 1 lb (500 g) loaves

Bread is such a versatile staple. You can make it with a variety of flours; it can be sweet or savory; fats can be added to change its flavor and texture. It can be served at every festival, plain or flavored with appropriate herbs, or spread with delicious herb butter or that season's preserves. It is a truly magickal food.

> 3 lb (1.5 kg) white bread flour, plus extra for dusting
> 2 teaspoons sugar
> 2 teaspoons salt
> 2 envelopes (14 g) instant yeast
> 1¼ cups (300 ml) cold water
> 1¼ cups (300 ml) boiling water
> Sunflower or vegetable oil, for greasing

Combine all the dry ingredients together in a large bowl. Put the cold water in a jug then add the boiling water. Pour the water into the bowl of dry ingredients and mix until you have a dough.

Turn out onto a floured surface and knead: press down hard and push it away from you then turn the dough clockwise and repeat the process. Knead for about 10 minutes until smooth and elastic, dusting your surface as needed to prevent the dough from sticking. Put the dough in a large bowl, cover with a warm damp tea towel, and place in a warm place to rise until at least doubled in size. (I leave mine in oven set to its lowest temperature).

Once the dough has risen, return to your floured surface and knead two or three times. Grease 1 lb (500 g) loaf pans or a large baking sheet with oil (I use a pastry brush). Using a sharp knife, cut off pieces of dough; you want them to half-fill your loaf pans. If you are using a baking sheet, form the dough into rounds. Once you are comfortable with bread-making you can make all sorts of shapes. Set aside in a warm place to proof for about 30 minutes, or until about doubled in size again.

Preheat your oven to its highest temperature and bake the bread for about 30 minutes. If you are baking in loaf pans, the bread will shrink from the sides of the pan when it is ready. If you are baking on a baking sheet, remove the bread from the oven after the 30 minutes and tap the bottom—it should sound hollow. Once your bread is baked, remove it from the oven and cover it with a tea towel until it has cooled.

WHITE SAUCE

If you know how to make a basic white sauce you can make so many different things. Make it in three thicknesses for different purposes—this is easy to do just by adding varying amounts of stock or milk. Add chopped parsley to a pouring sauce for an accompaniment to fish or ham; add nutmeg, salt, and pepper for a béchamel sauce to top lasagna; add breadcrumbs to a pouring sauce for a bread sauce; add cheese to a coating sauce for the sauce for macaroni or Cauliflower with Cheese (page 117); make a well-seasoned thick sauce to make a hearty chicken and mushroom pie filling. Knowing how to make a foundation sauce like this will enable to you to make sauces flavored with any herbs or spices for a whole variety of dishes. White sauce is usually made with milk but can also be made with stock.

	Extra thick	Coating sauce	Pouring sauce
Butter:	2 tablespoons (25 g)	2 tablespoons (25 g)	2 tablespoons (25 g)
Flour:	3 tablespoons (25 g)	3 tablespoons (25 g)	3 tablespoons (25 g)
Liquid:	½ cup (125 ml)	1 cup (250 ml)	2 cups (500 ml)
Other:	seasonings	seasonings	seasonings

Melt the butter in a saucepan over medium heat. Add flour and cook, whisking constantly, for a few minutes until you have a golden paste (a *roux*). Remove the pan from the heat and add a little of the liquid (milk or stock) and the seasonings suited to your dish, stirring briskly with a balloon whisk. Continue adding the liquid a little at a time to avoid lumps forming until you have a nice thick sauce. Taste and season further if you wish.

CUSTARD

Serves 4

1 tablespoon cornstarch
Generous 1¾ cups (450 ml) cold milk
1 egg, beaten
2 teaspoons sugar
A few drops vanilla extract

Using an electic hand mixer or stand mixer, blend the cornstarch with 2 tablespoons of the milk. Very gently heat the remaining milk in a saucepan over low heat (if you heat it too quickly the milk might burn). Pour the milk over the cornstarch mixture, then return the mixture to the pan. Bring to a boil then reduce the heat and simmer for 1 minute.

Remove from the heat and let the mixture cool slightly, then add the beaten egg. Return the pan to the heat and stir the mixture over low heat until it thickens, making sure it does not boil. This should only take 1–2 minutes.

Once the custard has thickened, add the sugar and vanilla and stir until dissolved. Serve hot or cold.

If serving cold or making ahead, transfer to a bowl and cover the surface of the custard with plastic wrap to avoid a skin forming.

MAYONNAISE

Makes approx. 1 cup (230 g)

2 egg yolks

1 teaspoon mustard powder or paste

1 teaspoon salt

1 cup (240 ml) white vinegar

Generous 1½ cups (375 ml) olive or sunflower oil,
        or a combination

In a blender, combine the egg yolks, mustard, salt, and vinegar and blend until the ingredients are thoroughly combined. Keeping the blender running, very slowly trickle in the oil, maintaining a continuous flow until all of the oil has been added. You should have an emulsified spread. Transfer to a clean jar and store in the refrigerator for up to a week.

BASIC RISOTTO

Serves 4 to 6

4¼–8½ cups (1–2 liters) chicken or vegetable stock
3 tablespoons (45 g) butter
1 onion, finely chopped
2 cups (350 g) Arborio rice
½ cup (125 ml) white wine
A good pinch of salt and freshly ground black pepper
    (or adjust to suit your taste)
Freshly grated Parmesan cheese, to serve

Place the stock in a large pot and bring to a boil, then reduce the heat to low.

In a large, heavy-bottomed sauté pan, slowly melt 2 tablespoons (30 g) of butter over low heat. Add the onion and cook slowly until transparent. Add the rice, salt, and pepper and stir until well mixed. Add the wine, stirring until the rice has absorbed the liquid.

Add a ladleful of the warm stock to the pan and stir until the stock has been absorbed. Repeat, adding a ladleful of stock at a time and stirring until absorbed, until the rice tender but still has some bite. The whole process will take about 20 minutes depending on the quality of the rice.

You can test if it is done by spooning a little rice into a bowl and shaking it lightly from side to side. The risotto should spread out very gently of its own accord. It should be creamy like oatmeal. If the rice just stands still, it is too dry so add a little more warm stock. If a puddle of liquid forms around the rice, you have added too much stock. Let the risotto sit for a few more seconds off the heat to absorb the excess stock.

Once cooked, turn off the heat and immediately add the remaining tablespoon (15 g) of butter and some Parmesan, stirring vigorously to combine. Taste and adjust the seasoning if needed. Transfer to serving plates and serve immediately with additional freshly grated Parmesan on top.

VARIATION: Near the end of cooking time, you can add cooked chicken, shrimp, or vegetables, depending on your recipe. For mushroom risotto, add the mushrooms at the beginning to allow the mushroom flavor to develop.

PERFECT RICE

Serves 2 to 4

This is my mom's way of making rice. and if you follow these directions, it will always turn out perfectly. Always use basmati rice; never use boil-in-the-bag or easy-cook rice. Allow ¼–½ cup (50–100 g) of uncooked rice per person (or more, if you prefer). The ratio to cook the rice is 1 part rice to 2 parts liquid.

I like to add cloves to my rice as it cooks because they ward off negative influences and I love the aromatic flavor, but you can flavor according to your ritual work. A cinnamon stick or some curry leaves are also nice flavorings. Cinnamon is a very powerful magickal spice. Like cloves, it represents protection but also spirituality, success, healing, power, psychic powers, lust, and love.

> 1 cup (200 g) basmati rice
> 2 cups (480 ml) water or chicken stock
> Boiling water, for soaking
> One or two cloves, or other flavorings (optional)

In a saucepan, bring the measured water or stock to a boil and set aside.

Meanwhile, put your rice into a large heatproof jug and cover with boiling water. Leave the rice to soak in the water for 5 minutes, stirring it once or twice. You will see the starch rising to the surface.

Drain the rice in a sieve and add it to the saucepan with the boiling liquid. There should only be 1 inch (2.5 cm) of liquid above the rice no matter what quantity you are cooking. My mother's favorite trick when adding the rice was to stand a spoon in the middle of the pot—if the spoon fell over there was too much water. (You can only do this if you are cooking a large quantity.)

Bring the stock and rice back to a boil, reduce the heat to its lowest setting, add any spices you might be using, and cover the pot with a tight-fitting lid. Do not stir and do not touch for at least 10 minutes.

After the 10 minutes, lift the lid and check the rice—there should be small air holes all over the surface. Replace the lid, turn off the heat, and leave the pot to stand for another 10 minutes, cooking in its own heat. It will then be ready to serve. If you added cloves, you can remove them before serving if you like.

PANCAKES

Serves 3

> 1⅔ cups (180 g) self-rising flour
> ½ teaspoon baking powder
> Scant ½ cup (90 g) sugar
> 1 teaspoon maple syrup
> 1 egg
> 1 cup (240 ml) milk
> Sunflower or vegetable oil, for frying

In a mixing bowl or large measuring jug, combine the flour, baking powder, and sugar and mix. Add the syrup (which gives the pancakes a nice golden color), egg, and ½ cup (120 ml) of the milk and stir to mix (at this stage, it will be lumpy with lots of loose flour). Add the remaining ½ cup (120 ml) of milk and mix until it is smooth, uniform, and fairly thick. At this point begin to beat the mixture using a whisk or fork. The mixture has the right consistency when it drips heavily and slowly from your fork or whisk. Set this batter aside in the refrigerator for about 10 minutes.

Heat a few drops of oil in a nonstick frying pan over medium heat. Using a paper towel or silicone brush, rub the oil around the base and sides of the pan. Remove the pancake mixture from the fridge and give it a stir. Drop 2–3-tablespoons of the batter into the hot pan (of course you can make your pancakes as big or as small as you like; mine are about 3 inches/7.5 cm). As soon as bubbles appear on the surface, use a spatula to flip the pancake over. If the pancake is too pale, raise the heat a little; if it is too brown, lower the heat. If the batter seems too thick, add a teaspoon more of milk and stir well. I usually cook four pancakes at a time in the pan after gauging the first for consistency and degree of heat. Your pancakes will cook in 1–2 minutes. Keep the cooked pancakes in a folded tea towel on a cooling rack until ready to eat.

CINNAMON PANCAKES

Cinnamon pancakes are quite easy to make and are a great addition to your table during Mabon. There are two ways to make these. The first is to add 1 teaspoon of cinnamon to the pancake batter above and cook as directed in the recipe. The second, and easiest, is to mix an equal ratio of cinnamon to confectioners' sugar together and then, once the pancakes are made, simply shake the mixture over the cooked pancakes.

SAMHAIN

Enfold us in your loving embrace
And keep us safe from harm.
Wherever we are, whatever place,
Keep us fed and warm.
The old ones who have gone before, return to grace our table,
Welcome say we, one and all, return if you are able.
Guide us, teach us, show us how to walk the sacred way,
That we may teach the ones who follow by the words we say.

CHAPTER TWO
SAMHAIN
(OCTOBER 31ST)

You will all be familiar with Halloween, when children (and adults!) dress up in scary clothes and do their best to "frighten" others into giving them treats. It is common at this time to carve a face into a hollowed-out pumpkin and then insert a candle into the cavity. When "guisers," as we call trick-or-treaters in Scotland, go calling at their neighbors' houses, they are expected to perform a song or poem, tell a story, or do something that merits a reward of fruit and nuts.

For pagans this time is known as Samhain (pronounced *sow-en*) and it is the first festival that we celebrate. At Samhain, the Goddess becomes the crone or wise one and the God lies in her womb waiting for the time of his rebirth at Yule.

In the farmer's year, Samhain used to mark the third and last harvest of the year, and the focus was on preparing for the winter. The survival of the farm animals would depend on the amount of fodder that had been cropped during the year and stored. Some animals were slaughtered for their meat, which might then have been hung and dried. Cropped vegetables that could be preserved would be prepared and safely stored to last through the winter.

Samhain is also the Celtic New Year and we believe that at this time the connection between the living and the dead is very strong. During this time we remember, show respect to, or ask for guidance from those who have passed over. We honor our ancestors and many leave altar offerings in the form of food and wine in tribute to dead relatives. Some pagans will set an extra place at the dinner table in memory of a family member who has passed over. Our loved ones can communicate with us in many ways and we must follow our instincts in order to receive their communication: you may suddenly remember the way they would say something to you or what they would have said; you may come across a photograph or a letter that you have not been aware of for some time; see or smell a loved one's favorite flower or scent, or find a book they loved, and this may cause you to react instinctively and remember them almost as though they were there with you. We are all different and our instincts react in a variety of ways. All you need to do is pay attention.

As pagans, we celebrate death as a part of life. Our celebrations involve gathering together various items that we use in our circle. While you might buy candy, nuts, and fruits for the children who come to your door, we gather candles of just the right colors and other accoutrements for our circle. We either work alone, with a friend or family member, or a coven.

SAMHAIN COLORS

The colors associated with Samhain are black, orange, red, brown, gold, and yellow.

SAMHAIN CRYSTALS

Crystals associated with Samhain are apache teardrop, jet, obsidian, and onyx.

SAMHAIN INCENSE

Incense can be made using dried apples, ground or grated nutmeg, dried sage, dried mint, and dried bay leaves. To any of these base ingredients you can add various gums or resins, such as gum Arabic or myrrh resin. Put your mixture into a small jar and label accordingly. This mixture can be sprinkled over charcoal disks.

SAMHAIN PURPOSE

This is a time for dispelling negative energy, invoking protection, and remembering our loved ones who have passed over. As with all rituals or ceremonies in the following pages, please feel free to amend them to suit your own needs, preferences, or purposes.

In some cases, where you may be called on to help someone or do a quick spell, you may only have time to wash your face and hands and take a few moments to think about what you are doing and why. But for normal rituals, you should make more of an effort by preparing as though you were going somewhere special. Take a shower or have a bath, wear clean, or ritual clothing, and if you have ritual jewelry wear that too. Once you are ready you can begin to gather the items that you need in your circle:

A tall, white or silver candle and holder to honor the Goddess
A tall, black, navy, or gold candle and holder to honor the God
If you are doing any spells during the ritual, you will need a tall, spell candle and holder of a
color that corresponds to your purpose
Four tea-light candleholders
Four white tea-light candles
Matches
A small dish of salt
A small bowl of water

A small bottle of essential oil
Some incense or a smudge stick
An athame or wand
A pentacle
An altar chalice or cup, filled with wine

You can add anything else that suits your particular requirements.

SAMHAIN RITUAL

Place the four small white tea-light candles at each corner of your room, or if you are able to have a circle place your candles starting at the east (which corresponds to the element of air), then the south (which corresponds to the element of fire), then the west (which corresponds to the element of water), and then the north (which corresponds to the element of earth). If you are unsure of the directions and do not have a compass, remember that the sun rises in the east and sets in the west. If you are still unsure, place your east candle to your left as you enter the room.

Place your two tall candles on your designated altar space, the Goddess candle to the left and the God candle to the right. If you are using a spell candle, place it in the center and your athame in front of it. Place the incense or smudge stick on your altar in the east quarter (air). Place the dish of water to the west (water) and place the salt to the north (earth). Place your pentacle on your altar space with your chalice or cup of wine.

Sit or kneel comfortably in front of your table or altar. Close your eyes and, as you breathe in, picture positive white light energy filling your body. As you breathe out, breathe away all negative energy. After some minutes, you will feel all the tension flowing away from your mind and body. Allow pure light energy to flow into and through your entire body, filling your sacred space, filling your room.

Say these words or create your own, and if you are working in a circle with any other person or people substitute "we" for "I" where necessary:

The circle is about to be cast,
Let none be here but of their own free will.

Pick up your matches and move to the east and light the east candle saying:

Here do I bring into the east light and air to illuminate this circle and bring it the breath of life.

The south candle is lit saying:

Here do I bring into the south light and fire to illuminate this circle and bring it warmth.

The west candle is lit saying:

> *Here do I bring into the west light and water to illuminate this circle and wash it clean.*

The north candle is lit saying:

> *Here do I bring into the north light and earth to illuminate this circle and build it in strength.*

Return to your altar and say:

> *This circle line I now prepare,*
> *Let no one enter should they dare.*
> *This sacred space I dedicate,*
> *Filled with love and never hate.*
> *So mote it be.*

Pick up your athame, wand, or use the index finger of your dominant hand to draw the circle in the air starting at the east, reaching the south, the west, then the north, and back to the east. Next touch the salt on your altar with your athame, wand, or index finger and say:

> *As salt is life, let it purify me so that I may use it to cleanse my body and spirit in honor of the God and Goddess.*

Put three pinches of salt in the water dish then raise your hand high, pointing your athame, wand, or index finger upwards, feeling the energy flowing into your arm. Put your athame, wand, or index finger into the water and stir three times, saying:

> *Salt is life, here is life, blessed be without strife, salt is life, here is life, blessed be without strife, salt is life, here is life, sacred be without strife.*

Sprinkle the salted water around the circle edge starting at the east, moving to the south, the west, and the north and back to the east. Return to your altar and put down the consecrated water. Light any altar candles and your incense then pick up the athame or wand or use your index finger to call the elemental guardians by drawing pentacles in the air, saying:

> *With air, fire, water, and earth I purify and charge you, east, hail guardians of the watchtower of the east, I invoke you [this could be a spirit guide, archangel, or your chosen God or Goddess], come by the air that is your breath, may you stand in strength ever watching over this circle.*
>
> *With fire, water, earth, and air I purify and charge you, south, hail guardians of the watchtower of the south, I invoke you [insert the name of the God or Goddess of your choice],*

come by the fire that is your spirit, may you stand in strength ever watching over this circle.

With water, earth, air, and fire I purify and charge you, west, hail guardians of the watchtower of the west, I invoke you [insert the name of the God or Goddess of your choice], come by the waters of your earthy womb that give us life, may you stand in strength ever watching over this circle.

With earth, air, fire, and water, I purify and charge you, north, hail guardians of the watchtower of the north, I invoke you [insert the name of the God or Goddess of your choice], come by the earth that is your body, may you stand in strength ever watching over this circle.

Take a drink from the chalice and focus your mind on the God and the Goddess. Then, standing in the Goddess position with your arms held high, invoke the Goddess energy into yourself and say:

Lady you have been known by many. I worship and adore you and invite you to join me in body and spirit. Be with me and guide me in the true ways.

Pick up your athame or wand or use your index finger and draw a pentacle in the air above you and below you and say:

You are here and I thank you for the gifts that you have given. I know that you only help those who help themselves. I ask:

Enfold us in your loving embrace
And keep us safe from harm.
Wherever we are, whatever place,
Keep us fed and warm.
The old ones who have gone before, return to grace our table,
Welcome say we, one and all, return if you are able.
Guide us, teach us, show us how to walk the sacred way,
That we may teach the ones who follow by the words we say.
An it harm none, do what thou will.
What we send forth will return thrice over, so we send it forth with light and love.
So mote it be.

Visualize your prayers and wishes rising to the moon Goddess. Pick up the chalice or cup in your left hand and the athame or wand in your right hand and hold them at eye level, then place the point of the athame or wand (or your index finger) into the wine and say:

> *May male and female be joined and let all be fruitful throughout the land. The food I eat is the blessing of the Gods and I remember those who have none. I am grateful for all I have been given and am open and ready to receive that which is still to come. So mote it be.*

> *We have met in love and friendship, let us part the same way, spreading the love from this circle outward to all, sharing it with those we meet. Lord and Lady my thanks to you for sharing this time with me, guarding and guiding me.*

> *Merry we meet, merry we part, merry we meet again. The circle will now be closed.*

Finish with:

> *Take for your use, eastern watchtower, any powers of air that have not been used.*
> *Take for your use, southern watchtower, any powers of fire that have not been used.*
> *Take for your use, western watchtower, any powers of water that have not been used.*
> *Take for your use, northern watchtower, any powers of earth that have not been used.*
> *The circle is now closed but the work continues.*
> *Let it harm none, so mote it be.*

SAMHAIN FOODS

Apples, oranges, nuts, grapes, beets, corn, pumpkins, squashes, turnips, cinnamon, nutmeg, allspice, mint, sage, ginger, pepper, rosemary, meats, rice, fowl, game dishes, rice dishes, mulled cider and wines, herbal teas, gingerbread, apple juice, and spicy punches.

SAMHAIN RECIPES

GARAM MASALA

Makes 1¾ cups (200 g)

In October, as the days get chillier, what is a better way to warm your bones a little than to spice things up a bit? Spices can be appropriate to your ritual work. Garam masala is the basis of many good curry dishes and this recipe will keep well in an airtight jar until you need it. One word of advice—do not buy the basic ingredients in the supermarket, since the selections and quantities are small. I recommend going to your local South Asian grocery store—you can find everything you need in larger quantities, which is more cost effective. (The products might have names that may be unfamiliar to you, but just ask for help!)

> 20 large black cardamom pods (or 10 green and 10 black)
> Scant ½ cup (60 g) black peppercorns
> ½ cup (60 g) coriander seeds
> Scant ½ cup (60 g) black cumin (*Bunium bulbocastanum*) ?
>   or caraway seeds
> 2 tablespoons (15 g) cloves
> 1½ tablespoons (15 g) ground cinnamon

Set a dry frying pan over medium heat and add the cardamom, peppercorns, coriander seeds, black cumin or caraway seeds, and cloves. Roast the seeds in a dry frying pan over medium heat until they turn a shade darker. Extract the seeds from the cardamom pods (discarding the pods) and coarsely grind the seeds in a mortar and pestle. Place in an airtight jar, add the toasted spices and cinnamon, and mix well. It will keep for a few months in a cool dark place.

SPICY BUTTERNUT SQUASH SOUP

Serves 4 to 6

1 tablespoon vegetable oil

1 onion, finely chopped

2 celery sticks, finely sliced

1 garlic clove, minced

1 teaspoon Garam Masala (page 45) or curry powder,
   plus extra to serve

1 medium butternut squash, peeled and cubed

4½ cups (1.1 liters) vegetable or chicken stock

Salt and freshly ground black pepper

Cilantro sprigs, to garnish (optional)

In a large soup pot, heat the oil over medium-low heat. Add the onion, celery, garlic, and garam masala or curry powder and sauté for 5–10 minutes, or until the vegetables are soft.

Add the butternut squash, mix well, and pour in the stock. Bring to a boil, lower the heat, and simmer for 20–30 minutes, or until the squash is soft.

Using a blender, food processor, or hand-held immersion blender, purée the soup until very smooth (or mash with a potato masher if you prefer a chunkier texture). Season with salt and pepper to taste.

Serve with a fine sprinkling of garam masala or curry powder on top, and a sprig of cilantro.

CHICKEN CURRY

Serves 4 to 6

Bright yellow turmeric—it cheers you up just to look at it! It is such an apt color for this season as the autumnal leaves start to fall. Lamb (stew slowly), shrimp (stir-fry quickly), or vegetables can be used instead of chicken in this dish. Use your favorite herbs to garnish. There's usually a pot of herbs growing on my windowsill. Any herbs can be in season on your kitchen windowsill.

> 6 tablespoons (90 g) butter
> 1½ teaspooons turmeric
> 1½ teaspoons Garam Masala (page 45)
> 1 teaspoon cayenne or crushed red pepper flakes, or to taste
> 1-inch (2.5 cm) piece of ginger, peeled and finely chopped
> 3 teaspoons salt
> 3 onions, finely chopped
> 4 garlic cloves, crushed
> 3 lb (1.5 kg) boneless, skinless chicken pieces
> 4 fresh tomatoes, peeled and chopped
> 2 tablespoons plain yogurt
> 2 tablespoons chopped fresh cilantro or sage

In a large sauté pan, melt the butter over medium heat. Add the spices and cook for 1 minute to release all their flavors. Add the onions and cook, stirring, until lightly browned, then add the garlic and chicken and stir a couple of times until the meat is thoroughly coated with the spice mixture. Put a lid on the pan, turn down the heat to low, and cook for 90 minutes, stirring occasionally.

Add the tomatoes and yogurt, stir well, and simmer for another 20 minutes. You should have a nice, thick curry but if it is too thin, leave the lid off and simmer, uncovered, for another 10–20 minutes until thickened. At the end of the cooking time and just before serving, sprinkle with cilantro or sage.

CHICKEN SOUP PIE (WITH HERB PASTRY) *Serves 4 to 6*

The name of this dish is not a mistake. And it has my one concession to convenience food—canned condensed chicken soup! This pie is one of our favorite quick meals. If you want to avoid using canned soup, make an extra thick white sauce (see page 31), season it well, and use it to bind together all the cooked ingredients of the pie.

Tarragon traditionally pairs with chicken and its magickal properties are calming and nurturing. This herb is perfect to add to this pie since it is real comfort food. You can of course use your favorite herbs or use ones that complement your ritual or spell work. Black pepper and nutmeg would also be appropriate Samhain spices that would go well with this dish.

For a variation, you can sprinkle a handful of sesame seeds, pumpkin seeds, or pine nuts over the pastry after you have brushed it with the egg or milk. Nuts and seeds are seasonal and appropriate for Samhain.

1 leek

1 tablespoon olive oil

4 tablespoons (60 g) butter, plus extra if needed

1 garlic clove, crushed

6–8 oz (180–250 g) leftover cooked chicken pieces or
    boneless chicken breasts, diced

14 oz (400 g) can condensed chicken soup

Milk or cream, if needed

8 oz (250 g) Shortcrust Pastry dough (page 28)

Up to 3 oz (90 g) of coarsely chopped herbs to suit your ritual or
    spell work (tarragon, sage, and rosemary go well with chicken)

1 tablespoon milk or 1 beaten egg

Ground black pepper or nutmeg (optional)

Cut the leek just on the edge of the white part (the green end can be cleaned, diced, and stored in the freezer to use later in soups). Cut the white of the leek lengthwise and then cut both pieces in half again. Dice the split leek, transfer to a colander, and rinse under cold running water to remove any soil, then set aside to drain.

In a large skillet, warm the olive oil over low heat. Add the butter and allow it to melt, then add the garlic and drained leek. Cook the garlic and leek very slowly for several minutes until they are soft, but do not let them brown.

If you are using fresh chicken breasts, use a separate pan to fry the chunks in butter until cooked through. When the leek is soft, add the cooked chicken. Stir the chicken and leek mixture until well mixed, then add the can of condensed chicken soup. Mix again so that the soup is well incorporated and then continue to simmer the mixture for a few minutes until slightly thickened. (If you feel that the mixture is too thick, you can mix in a little milk or cream.) Spoon into a deep casserole dish and set aside.

Preheat the oven to 350°F (180°C).

On a floured surface, roll the shortcrust pastry into a ball. Sprinkle your chosen herbs and black pepper over your work surface, then roll the pastry ball over and over through your herbs until they are thoroughly mixed into the pastry. Roll the pastry out to a thickness of about ⅛ inch (3 mm), just a little larger than your casserole dish, to use as a lid for the pie (there is no base). Cover the dish with the pastry, folding it slightly over the edges of the dish and trimming any excess. Brush the top with the milk or beaten egg.

Bake the pie for 20–30 minutes until the pastry is cooked and nicely browned.

ROAST HAM WITH ROSEMARY

Serves 6

Rosemary is one of my favorite herbs and smells so wonderful in a roast dinner. Rosemary is a perfect Samhain herb: an evergreen shrub that brings protection.

>2–3 lb (1–1.5 kg) boneless ham (cured or uncured)
>2 tablespoons olive oil
>2 tablespoons dried rosemary or several sprigs of fresh rosemary

Preheat the oven to 350°F (180°C). Rinse the ham under cold water, pat dry, then place in a roasting pan and drizzle with the olive oil. Sprinkle the dried or fresh rosemary over the ham and then cover with foil.

Roast the ham in the oven for 1 hour. Remove from the oven and pierce with a sharp, pointed knife. If the meat is ready the knife will slide fairly easily into the meat; when it is withdrawn touch the tip of the knife to the back of your hand—if it is hot then the meat is likely to be ready. Or you can check the temperature using a meat thermometer—the center of the ham should be 160°F (70°C). If it is not heated through, baste the ham with the juices in the pan and put it back in the oven for a further 10–30 minutes, checking from time to time.

Remove the ham from the oven and leave it to rest for about 10 minutes before slicing. If the ham is not being served immediately, let it cool before storing in the refrigerator. Hot or cold, this ham is lovely with Cauliflower with Cheese (page 117).

ROAST PORK TENDERLOIN WITH ORANGE AND ONION SAUCE

Serves 4

Oranges and tangerines are traditionally given as rewards to your visiting "guisers" (trick-or-treaters). Orange is the color of this month. I always love the autumnal colors and the bright squashes and pumpkins that are ready in this season. There is color everywhere if you look for it!

2 pork tenderloins

2 tablespoons olive oil

2 fresh thyme sprigs

2 tablespoons finely chopped fresh parsley

2 tablespoons (30 g) unsalted butter

½ cup (125 ml) freshly squeezed orange juice

½ cup (125 ml) Meat Stock (page 25) or other stock

Orange and Onion Sauce

5 tablespoons olive oil

1 white onion, thinly sliced

Pinch of sugar

6 tablespoons balsamic vinegar

6 tablespoons white wine vinegar

1 cup (240 ml) fresh orange juice

Grated zest of 1 orange

A good pinch of salt and freshly ground pepper

Preheat the oven to 350°F (180°C). Place the tenderloins in a roasting pan and cover with the olive oil, thyme, parsley, butter, fresh orange juice, and stock, then cover with a lid or foil. Bake for about 45 minutes until tender. Remove the pan from the oven, uncover the pork, then bake for a further 30 minutes to brown the top.

Meanwhile, make the sauce: Heat the olive oil in a nonstick frying pan over low heat, then add the onion and sugar and stir frequently until the onion turns a nice golden color. Add both vinegars, the orange juice and zest, and salt and pepper and cook slowly for 20–30 minutes, or until the liquid has evaporated and the onions are soft. Keep the sauce warm until ready to serve.

Remove the pork from the oven and carefully pierce the meat with a knife. If the liquid is clear and the point of the knife is hot, it is ready. If the liquid is pink or red, it is not cooked—leave it in the oven for a few more minutes. Once cooked, remove from the oven and leave the pork to rest for about 10 minutes, then slice and place on a serving platter. Drizzle with the sauce and serve.

BUBBLE AND SQUEAK

Serves 4 to 6

In case you don't know, this dish of potatoes, onions, and cabbage, came about to use up leftover vegetables after a roast dinner. You can add any magickal herbs and/or spices suited to your ritual or spell work while the ingredients are frying or add them to the cooking water of the cabbage or potatoes. A bit of fried bacon is also a nice addition, or you can use up any leftover meat or vegetables from your refrigerator. It is a great midweek meal.

> 2 lb (900 g) potatoes, peeled
> 6 tablespoons (90 g) butter, plus a little extra for the cabbage
> 2 medium onions, diced
> 1 tablespoon of olive oil
> 1 lb (450 g) cabbage, cleancd and chopped
> Salt and freshly ground black pepper
> Vegetable oil, for shallow-frying (optional)

Boil the potatoes until a knife pierces them without difficulty (about 20 minutes). When they are ready, drain and roughly mash them with the butter and add salt and pepper to taste.

Heat the olive oil in a frying pan over medium heat and gently fry the onions for several minutes until they are soft but not brown.

While the onions are cooking, boil the cabbage until it is tender. When it is cooked, drain and toss with a little butter.

Combine all of the vegetables in a large pot and place over medium heat. Season to taste, then cook, stirring, for a few minutes until heated through and well combined. Alternatively, form the vegetable mixture into small patties and shallow-fry in oil until heated through and browned on both sides.

CAULIFLOWER WITH RICE

Serves 4 to 6

4 tablespoons (60 g) butter
1 cauliflower, cut into florets
Buttermilk or plain yogurt, to serve
Your favorite herb or a salad, to serve

Perfect Rice
1 cup (200 g) basmati rice
2 cups (480 ml) water or stock
Boiling water, for soaking
1 or 2 cloves (optional)

In a frying pan, melt the butter over medium-high heat and shallow fry the cauliflower until browned all over.

Meanwhile, start the rice: Bring the measured water or stock to a boil in a stockpot and set aside. Put the rice into a large heatproof jug and cover with boiling water. Leave the rice to soak in the water for 5 minutes, stirring it once or twice. You will see the starch rising to the surface.

Drain the rice in a sieve, add it to the stockpot with the boiling liquid, then add the browned cauliflower on top. One or two cloves will help to ward off negative influences as well as tasting good! Bring to a boil, reduce the heat to its lowest setting, and cover with a tight-fitting lid. Do not stir and do not touch for at least 10 minutes.

After the 10 minutes, lift the lid and check the rice—there should be small air holes all over the surface. Replace the lid, turn off the heat, and leave the rice to stand for another 10 minutes, cooking in its own heat. If you added cloves, you can remove them before serving.

To serve, transfer the cauliflower and rice to bowls, top with a generous helping of buttermilk or plain yogurt, and garnish with your favorite herb or serve with salad on the side.

POTATO SALAD WITH ROSEMARY AND GARLIC

Serves 4

4 medium potatoes (approx. 1 lb/450 g), peeled

1 sprig fresh rosemary, needles only, coarsely chopped
   (or more, if you prefer)

2 garlic cloves, crushed

Approx. ½ cup (115 g) Mayonnaise (page 33)

Salt and freshly ground black pepper

Boil the potatoes until soft and set aside to cool. Once cooled, roughly chop them into bite-size pieces and transfer to a bowl.

Add the rosemary and garlic to the potatoes and gently mix. Gently stir in the mayonnaise, a tablespoon at a time, until you have your desired consistency. Season to taste with salt and pepper. Serve immediately, or store in the refrigerator for later.

BEETS

Beets are full of vitamin C and antioxidants—very good for healing. And they are quite easy to grow, or find in farmer's markets or local grocery stores.

I love it when I find fresh raw beets in my local grocery store and I get to take home a large bagful. I have had strange looks from cashiers, since I am sure they are wondering why I could possibly want so much! To be honest, the best part for me is peeling the cooked beets and I giggle like a child when I do. I am sure there must be some Freudian interpretation for this peculiar delight, but wait until you experience it before making any judgements!

Let's start with the raw root. Raw beets are really hard and quite dark and unappealing to the eye, but take them home and cook them—you won't be disappointed. Put them in a large pot, cover with water, and let them boil for an hour. To test whether they are done, pierce one with a sharp knife—if it goes through smoothly then it is ready. Take the pot to the sink and set under cold running water until the water in the pot is cool, then set aside for about 10 minutes until the beets are cool enough to handle. Now for the fun part: pick up one of the beets, squeeze hard over the sink, and if they are cooked properly the skin will slip off and chances are the beet will scoot around the sink! Continue until all the beets are skinned, then cut off the tops and bottoms using a sharp knife if they haven't already broken off (you can also cut away any bruised or damaged bits). Cooked beets are delicious as they are, but you now have the basis of any number of recipes, like soups, salads, pickles, and chutneys. You can also freeze cooked sliced or grated beets in individual portions for later use.

PICKLED BEETS

Makes 2–3 pint-size (450 g) jars

This recipe is pretty versatile in its flavoring, though I recommend choosing spices that go with beet's earthy sweetness, such as cinnamom, ginger, mustard seed, cloves, and black pepper.

> 1 lb (450 g) cooked beets (sliced, diced, or left whole—your preference)
> Approx. 2 cups (480 ml) vinegar (any variety is fine), or enough to
>   cover the beets
> Spices (here is a nice combination: 1 cinnamon stick, 2–3 cloves,
>   2–3 bay leaves, 5 black peppercorns, and a good pinch of salt)
> 1 teaspoon granulated or brown sugar (your preference)

Wash your pickle jars and then submerge them in a pot of hot water. Bring to a boil and boil vigorously for 10 minutes to sterilize the jars.

In a large soup pot, bring to a boil enough vinegar to cover your cooked beets. Add your chosen spices and the sugar to the pot. Boil everything together for a few minutes. Taste it and adjust the seasoning as needed to suit your own taste; it should be strongly flavored so the beets can slowly absorb this flavor.

Ladle your cooked beets into the hot sterilized jars and cover with the spiced vinegar. Allow to cool, then cover and transfer to the refrigerator. Allow a few days for the flavors to develop before eating, and use within 2 months.

VARIATION: To make a spicy version, slice the cooked beets and place into clean jars. Add the flavorings of your choice (such as 2–3 red, green, or black peppercorns, 2–3 juniper berries or cardamom, and 1 garlic clove) along with 1 whole uncut chili per jar. Fill the jar with good vinegar so that no flesh is exposed. Cover and refrigerate as above.

NOTE: You can use ready-cooked beets, but this is what I consider to be for emergency use only, i.e., when I have run out of my pickled stock in my pantry or I can't find any fresh ones. Open the package and rinse well before using.

ROASTED CARROTS

Serves 6

If you have grown your own late-sown carrots you should be harvesting them now and storing them for the winter. Roasted carrots really are a surprise—they taste truly magickal and, like any of the foods in this book, can be made incorporating the herbs and spices that will suit your ritual work. Nutmeg and rosemary work very well from a flavor point of view. Nutmeg is useful in rituals for health, wealth, good fortune, and for boosting other herbs or spices in spell work; rosemary is good for protection, which is appropriate during Samhain.

> 12 medium-sized carrots, trimmed (you can leave them whole
> or slice them diagonally)
> Olive oil, for drizzling
> ½ tablespoon brown sugar
> Herbs and/or spices to suit your magickal or ritual work (optional)

Preheat the oven to 350°F (180°C). Place the carrots on a large baking sheet, drizzle with olive oil, and roast them for 30 minutes until just tender.

Remove the carrots from the oven, sprinkle with the brown sugar and any herbs and/or spices, and mix to coat them well.

Increase the oven temperature to 400°F (200°C), then roast the carrots for another 10 minutes before serving.

UPSIDE DOWN APPLE PIE

Serves 4 to 6

This is similar to traditional apple pie; however, the pie is cooked without a base. The pastry lid becomes the base when the pie is turned upside down after baking. That cinnamon-apple-nutmeg smell as it cooks ... wonderful!

> ½ portion Shortcrust Pastry (page 28)
> 1 tablespoon (15 g) butter
> ⅓ cup (60 g) mixed dried fruit (like currants, raisins, and
>   dried citrus peel)
> A handful of nuts (like pecans, pistachios, hazelnuts, or walnuts),
>   crushed
> 4 firm, tart cooking apples (Bramley apples if you can get them),
>   peeled, cored, and diced
> 2 tablespoons brown sugar (dark or light)
> A good pinch of cinnamon
> A good pinch of nutmeg
> Whipped cream or Custard (page 32) to serve

Preheat the oven to 380°F (190°C). Roll out the shortcrust pastry to an 8-inch (20 cm) round with a thickness of about ⅛ inch (3 mm). Generously grease the bottom of an 8-inch (20 cm) pie dish with the butter and scatter with the dried fruit, nuts, and diced apples. Sprinkle the sugar and spices over the apples and top with the pastry round.

Bake the pie for 30 minutes. Remove from the oven and cool slightly. Place a serving plate on top of the pie dish and carefully flip the pie over onto the plate. Top with whipped cream or custard and serve.

CINNAMON BREAD

Makes 1 loaf or 4–8 rolls

Dough
2¼ cups (250 g) self-rising flour

2 tablespoons sugar

A pinch of salt

1 teaspoon cinnamon

1 egg

Scant 1¼ cups (285 ml) milk

¼ cup (60 ml) sunflower oil

Topping
2 tablespoons brown sugar

1 teaspoon all-purpose flour

A pinch of ground cinnamon

1 teaspoon melted butter

Preheat the oven to 400°F (200°C) and line a baking sheet with parchment paper.

Combine all the dry ingredients together in a large bowl. Slowly mix in the water and oil until a rough dough forms.

Turn out onto a floured surface and turn the dough a few times until it comes together. Form it into a loaf or rolls (whichever you prefer) and space out on the lined baking sheet.

To make the topping, mix the sugar, flour, and cinnamon together. Brush the loaf or rolls with the melted butter then sprinkle with the dry mixture.

If making a loaf, bake for 20–25 minutes. To check if it is done, tap the the bottom—it should sound hollow. If making rolls, bake for 10–15 minutes, or until golden.

LEMON AND ROSEMARY COOKIES *Makes approx. 15*

You can vary this recipe using herbs to suit your ritual or spell work.

> 6 tablespoons (90 g) butter, plus extra for greasing
> Generous 2 tablespoons (30 g) sugar, plus extra for sprinkling
> Generous 1 cup (125 g) self-rising flour, plus extra for dusting
> 1½ cups (180 g) confectioners' sugar
> 1 sprig of fresh rosemary (about 4 inches/10 cm long), needles only,
>   coarsely chopped
> Freshly squeezed juice of ½ lemon
> 2 teaspoons water

Using an electic hand mixer or stand mixer, cream together the butter and sugar in a bowl. Sieve the flour and confectioners' sugar together and gradually mix into the butter and sugar. Add the chopped rosemary, lemon juice, and water and mix until the mixture forms a firm dough.

Preheat the oven to 350°F (180°C). Grease and lightly flour a baking sheet.

Roll out the dough to a thickness of about ⅛ inch (3 mm), cut into rounds or other shapes, and sprinkle them with sugar. Space out your cookies on the baking sheet and bake on the middle rack of the oven for 10 minutes, or until golden.

Remove from the oven and leave the cookies to cool, then store in an airtight container. Mine have never lasted longer than the day they are baked—they are eaten immediately!

CHOCOLATE APPLES

Serves 6

6 lollipop sticks
6 large dessert apples (approx. 8 oz each), washed and dried
½ cup (60 g) pecans or pistachios
10½ oz (300 g) milk chocolate

Push the lollipop sticks two-thirds of the way through the bottom core of each apple and set aside. Line a baking sheet with parchment paper.

Coarsely chop the nuts in a food processor or crush with the end of a rolling pin or a mortar and pestle (the nuts should be roughly broken rather than ground). Set aside in a bowl.

Place the chocolate in a heatproof bowl that will sit comfortably on top of a saucepan half-filled with water. Place the pan over low heat and slowly melt the chocolate, stirring occasionally. Once melted fully, remove the bowl from the pan and dip each apple into the chocolate, turning to coat, then coat with the chopped nuts. Place your coated apples on the baking sheet to harden before eating.

CANDIED APPLES

Serves 6

6 lollipop sticks
6 large dessert apples (approx. 8 oz each), washed and dried
½ cup (100 g) sugar
½ cup (125 ml) golden or maple syrup
½ teaspoon vanilla extract

Push the lollipop sticks two-thirds of the way through the bottom core of each apple and set aside. Line a baking sheet with parchment paper.

In a saucepan, combine the sugar and syrup over medium heat. Stirring constantly, bring to a rolling boil (do not let this burn). Every 5 minutes or so, use a teaspoon to drop a tiny amount of the mixture onto a cold, wet place. It is ready when it sets on the plate and is not runny. If you have a cooking thermometer, cook the mixture until it reaches 300°F (150°C).

Remove the pot from the heat and mix in the vanilla extract. Carefully dip each apple into the hot syrup, coating them evenly. Place the apples upside down (stick pointing up) on the baking sheet to harden before eating.

CIDER PUNCH

Serves 4

Great for Halloween parties, though not for the kids (you could make an alcohol-free version using apple juice).

> 4¼ cups (1 liter) alcoholic apple cider
> Juice of ½ lemon
> 2 tablespoons brown sugar
> 1 cinnamon stick
> A few cloves (no more than 5)
> 1 inch (2.5 cm) piece fresh ginger, peeled and bruised
> Fresh nutmeg, to serve

In a large stockpot, combine the cider, lemon juice, and sugar and place over low heat until the sugar has dissolved. Tie the spices together in a piece of cheesecloth, drop it into the pot, and simmer for 30 minutes. Serve hot in mugs with a grating of nutmeg on top.

PUMPKIN

Any of the following recipes will make good use of your Halloween pumpkin innards after making your jack-o'-lantern! Beware though—some pumpkins that are sold in the supermarkets in October are fine for using as lanterns but might contain disappointingly little flesh inside, and what is there could be a bit fibrous and watery. You could also use winter squashes such as butternut, onion, or acorn in any of these recipes; they have firm flesh and a bit more flavor. The seeds can be cleaned and roasted and are delicious as a snack or a garnish.

For a versatile mash, peel, slice and then steam or boil your pumpkin or squash, or simply slice and roast until soft (once roasted, you can peel away the cooked skin easily). A y-shaped peeler is the easiest to use on squashes. Mash the flesh to use in a variety of recipes, including some of the those given here.

PUMPKIN SOUP

Serves 4 to 6

4 lb (1.75 kg) pumpkin, peeled and chopped
2 apples (any kind will do), coarsely chopped
2 onions, coarsely chopped
2½ cups (600 ml) chicken or vegetable stock
1 teaspoon ground nutmeg, plus extra to serve
2½ cups (600 ml) water
Salt and freshly ground black pepper, to taste
Cream, to serve

Place all of the ingredients in a large pot and bring to a boil over high heat. Turn the heat to low, cover, and simmer for 40 minutes, or until the pumpkin is tender. Set aside to cool a little, then blend using a food processor, blender, or hand-held immersion blender until smooth. Taste and adjust the seasoning to your liking. Garnish with a drizzle of cream and a sprinkle of nutmeg.

Pumpkin Cheesecake

Serves 4 to 6

6 oz (180 g) vanilla cookies or graham crackers, crushed,
    or leftover sponge cake, crumbled

4 tablespoons (60 g) unsalted butter, softened, plus extra for greasing

½ cup (60 g) dried pumpkin seeds

1 lb (500 g) cream cheese, softened

Scant ⅔ cup (125 g) organic granulated sugar

1 teaspoon vanilla extract

3 eggs

1 teaspoon ground cinnamon

½ teaspoon ground nutmeg

1 cup (245 g) mashed cooked pumpkin, cold (see page 65)

In a bowl, combine the cookies or cake, butter, and the pumpkin seeds (reserving some for decoration). Mix well using a spatula or spoon. Grease a 9-inch (23 cm) springform cake pan and press the mixture into the base. Set aside.

Preheat the oven to 325°F (170°C). Using an electic hand mixer or stand mixer, mix the cream cheese, sugar, and vanilla extract at medium speed until well blended. Add the eggs, spices, and mashed pumpkin and mix again. Spread this mixture over the base and sprinkle the reserved seeds over the top.

Bake for 1 hour, until set. Test it by gently shaking the pan—if it is set, the very center will jiggle slightly. If it is not set, bake for a few more minutes then test again.

Leave the cheesecake to cool before transferring to a serving plate. Chill before serving.

PUMPKIN SEED BREAD

Makes 1 loaf

  3 lb (1.5 kg) white bread flour, plus extra for dusting

  2 teaspoons sugar (optional, but the sugar will create a nice crust)

  2 teaspoons salt

  2 envelopes (14 g) instant yeast

  2 tablespoons pumpkin seeds

  1¼ cups (300 ml) cold water

  1¼ cups (300 ml) boiling water

  Vegetable oil, for greasing

Follow the method on page 30 to make 1 loaf or round.

PUMPKIN MUFFINS

Makes 12

Don't over-mix the muffins or they will be tough. Combine the ingredients thoroughly but quickly.

Generous 1 cup (125 g) self-rising flour, sifted
A pinch of salt
A pinch of ground cinnamon
Scant ½ cup (90 g) sugar, plus extra for sprinkling
4 tablespoons (60 g) butter
1 egg
1 cup (245 g) mashed cooked pumpkin, cold (see page 65)
2 teaspoons milk
Dried pumpkin seeds, to garnish

Preheat the oven to 350°F (180°C). Place the flour, salt, and cinnamon in a bowl and set aside. In another bowl, beat the sugar and butter using an electric hand mixer or whisk until light and fluffy, then add the egg, pumpkin, and milk and mix well. Fold the dry ingredients into the wet ingredients until combined.

Place paper liners in the holes of a muffin tray and fill each about third-quarters full with the batter (do not overfill). Top the muffins with dried pumpkin seeds and a fine sprinkling of sugar, then bake for 20 minutes, or until golden brown and a toothpick inserted into the center comes out clean.

PUMPKIN COOKIES

Makes appprox. 15

9 tablespoons (125 g) butter, plus extra for greasing

Scant 1 cup (180 g) sugar

1 egg

1 cup (245 g) mashed cooked pumpkin, cold (see page 65)

1 teaspoon vanilla extract

2¼ cups (250 g) self-rising flour

1 teaspoon ground nutmeg

1 teaspoon ground cinnamon

A pinch of salt

Scant ½ cup (50 g) walnuts, chopped

1 cup (170 g) chocolate chips

Preheat the oven to 350°F (180°C). In a mixing bowl, cream together the butter and sugar using an electric hand mixer or whisk, then add the egg and mix well. Add the pumpkin and vanilla and mix.

In another bowl, mix together the flour, spices, and salt, then add to the pumpkin mixture, stirring well. Once combined, add the nuts and chocolate chips and mix again.

Grease a baking sheet. Drop tablespoonfuls of the dough onto the baking sheet, leaving about ½ inch (1 cm) between each cookie. Bake for 10–15 minutes, or until golden.

ORANGE JELLO TRIFLE

Serves 4

2 mandarins or clementines, peeled and cut into segments (make
　　sure there is no pith), or a 14 oz (400 g) can mandarin
　　slices, drained
4 tablespoons orange liqueur
3½ oz (100 g) lady fingers (Savoiardi cookies; about ½ package),
　　or leftover spongecake pieces
3 oz (85 g) package orange jello
Cold water
1 portion Custard (page 32), chilled
½ cup (120 ml) heavy cream, whipped

Soak the mandarin or clementines in 2 tablespoons of the orange liqueur.

Mix the jello according to the package instructions, substituting 2 tablespoons of the cold water
with the remaining 2 tablespoons of the orange liqueur. Set aside.

Arrange the cookies or cake pieces in the bottom and around the sides of a trifle dish or a large
glass bowl (I like to leave space betwee them on the sides so you can see the other ingredients).
Pour in half of the fruit and their liquid. Top with the jello mixture and put in the refrigerator
until completely set.

Once the jello has set, pour the cooled custard on top. Top the custard layer with the whipped
cream. Put the trifle back in the refrigerator to chill completely. When you are ready to serve,
decorate the top with the rest of the liqueur-soaked oranges.

YULE

Old friendships renewed, and loved ones return,
Good feelings imbued, as our fires they burn,
Our future as bright, as the Lady's light.
The Sun God is born, and our hearths are warm,
With loved ones we share our love and our fayre.

CHAPTER THREE

YULE

(YULE: DECEMBER 21ST OR 22ND; CHRISTMAS: DECEMBER 25TH)

Yule is the pagan midwinter festival. Most cultures have a midwinter festival from late December to mid-January. It is a time of sharing and loving; gifts are exchanged and friends and family join together and share the best food they can afford. And of course Christians celebrate the birth of Christ at this time. In many counties, the contemporary Christmastide or Yuletide traditions involve the decoration of a tree, giving of gifts, lighting of candles or lights, delicious food, singing, dancing, family gatherings, and reunions with friends.

Pagans celebrate Yule on December 21st or 22nd. This is the winter solstice—the shortest day and the longest night of the year—the last feast before winter sets in. In times past, people could not be sure if they would survive the winter, so this was a time of great preparation for the lean months ahead. Their animals would be slaughtered and preserved because there might be nothing on which to feed them during the winter months; this would also ensure fresh meat for Yule.

The Yule log, a long cake covered with chocolate and decorated with holly and red berries, is inspired by the pagan Yule log, which was cut from an oak or ash tree and burned to chase away the cold of winter and invite the warmth of summer. The Yule log was never allowed to burn entirely through and was kept from one year to the next, so that each new Yule log could be lit from the previous one.

December 21st consists of the longest night and the shortest day of the year, but from this date on the daylight grows longer. Mother Earth gives birth to the Sun God and, with his return, light and warmth return to the earth. This is a time to look forward to the coming spring and to think about your plans for the future.

It is a time to look in your pantry and break open the summer's jams, chutneys, and conserves and homemade wines and beers!

YULE COLORS

Colors associated with Yule are red, white, green, gold, and silver.

YULE CRYSTALS

Crystals associated with Yule are bloodstone, sunstone, quartz, rutilated quartz, goldstone, and citrine.

YULE INCENSE

Incense for Yule can be made by using sage, cinnamon, nutmeg, caraway, cloves, and allspice. To any of these base ingredients you can add various gums or resins, such as gum Arabic or myrrh resin. Put your mixture into a small jar and label accordingly. This mixture can be sprinkled over charcoal disks.

YULE PURPOSE

Yule is a particularly good time to carry out spells for reunions and prosperity for the coming year. As with all rituals or ceremonies in the following pages, please feel free to amend them to suit your own needs, preferences, or purposes.

YULE RITUAL

Please refer to the instructions on page 41 (Samhain Ritual) to set up your circle. Then say these words or create your own:
> *The circle is about to be cast.*
> *Let none be here but of their own free will.*

Pick up your matches and move to the east and light the east candle saying:
> *Here do I bring into the east light and air to illuminate this circle and bring it the breath of life.*

The south candle is lit saying:
> *Here do I bring into the south light and fire to illuminate this circle and bring it warmth.*

The west candle is lit saying:
> *Here do I bring into the west light and water to illuminate this circle and wash it clean.*

The north candle is lit saying:

> *Here do I bring into the north light and earth to illuminate this circle and build it in strength.*

Return to your altar and say:

> *This circle line I now prepare,*
> *Let no one enter should they dare.*
> *This sacred space I dedicate,*
> *Filled with love and never hate.*
> *So mote it be.*

Pick up your athame or wand or use the index finger of your dominant hand and draw a circle in the air, starting at the east, reaching the south, the west, then the north, and back to the east. Next touch the salt on your altar with your athame, wand, or index finger and say:

> *As salt is life, let it purify me so that I may use it to cleanse my body and spirit in honor of the God and Goddess.*

Put three pinches of salt in the water dish then raise your hand high pointing your athame, wand, or index finger upwards, feeling the energy flowing into your arm. Put your athame, wand, or index finger into the water and stir three times, saying:

> *Salt is life, here is life, blessed be without strife, salt is life, here is life, blessed be without strife, salt is life, here is life, sacred be without strife.*

Sprinkle the salted water around the circle edge starting at the east, moving to the south, the west, the north, and then back to the east. Return to your altar and put down the consecrated water. Light any altar candles and your incense then pick up your athame or wand or use your finger to call the elemental guardians by drawing pentacles in the air saying:

> *With air, fire, water, and earth, I purify and charge you, east, hail guardians of the watchtower of the east, I invoke you [insert the name of the God or Goddess of your choice], come by the air that is your breath, may you stand in strength ever watching over this circle.*

> *With fire, water, earth, and air, I purify and charge you, south, hail guardians of the watchtower of the south, I invoke you [insert the name of the God or Goddess of your choice], come by the fire that is your spirit, may you stand in strength ever watching over this circle.*

With water, earth, air, and fire, I purify and charge you, west, hail guardians of the watchtower of the west, I invoke you [insert the name of the God or Goddess of your choice], come by the waters of your earthy womb that give us life, may you stand in strength ever watching over this circle.

With earth, air, fire, water, I purify and charge you, north, hail guardians of the watchtower of the north, I invoke you [insert the name of the God or Goddess of your choice], come by the earth that is your body, may you stand in strength ever watching over this circle.

Take a drink from the chalice and focus your mind on the God and the Goddess. Then, standing in the Goddess position with your arms held high, invoke the Goddess energy into yourself and say:

Lady you have been known by many. I worship and adore you and invite you to join me in body and spirit. Be with me and guide me in the true ways.

Pick up your athame or wand, or use your index finger, and draw a pentacle in the air above you and below you and say:

You are here and I thank you for the gifts that you have given. I know that you only help those who help themselves. I ask:

Old friendships renewed, and loved ones return,
Good feelings imbued, as our fires they burn,
Our future as bright, as the Lady's light.
The Sun God is born, and our hearths are warm,
With loved ones we share our love and our fayre.
An it harm none do what thou will.
What we send forth will return thrice over, so we send it forth with light and love.
So mote it be.

Visualize your prayers and wishes rising to the moon Goddess. Pick up the chalice or cup in your left hand and the athame or wand in your right hand and hold them at eye level, then place the point of the athame or wand or your index finger into the wine and say:

May male and female be joined and let all be fruitful throughout the land.
The food I eat is the blessing of the Gods and I remember those who have none. I am grateful for all I have been given and am open and ready to receive that which is still to come.
So mote it be.

We have met in love and friendship, let us part the same way, spreading the love from this
circle outward to all, sharing it with those we meet.
Lord and Lady my thanks to you for sharing this time with me, guarding and guiding me.
Merry we meet, merry we part, merry we meet again.
The circle will now be closed.

Finish with:

Take for your use, eastern watchtower, any powers of air that have not been used.
Take for your use, southern watchtower, any powers of fire that have not been used.
Take for your use, western watchtower, any powers of water that have not been used.
Take for your use, northern watchtower, any powers of earth that have not been used.
The circle is now closed but the work continues.
An it harm none, so mote it be.

YULE FOODS

Chestnuts, nuts, pomegranates, grapes, potatoes, sprouts, parsnips, rutabaga, beets, cinnamon, nutmeg, caraway, cloves, allspice, sage, mulled wine, ginger wine, brandy, sherry, beers, wassail, spiced teas.

YULE RECIPES

CHICKEN AND LEEK SOUP

Serves 4 to 6

4¼ cups (1 liter) chicken stock

4¼ cups (1 liter) water

2 leeks, cleaned and diced into 1-inch (2.5 cm) pieces

6 carrots, peeled and grated

2½ tablespoons long-grain rice

Salt and freshly ground black pepper

Parsley, finely chopped, to garnish

Put the chicken stock and measured water into a large soup pot over high heat, cover with a lid, and bring to a boil.

Add the leeks, carrots, and rice to the pot, stir, and bring back to a boil. Reduce the heat to low, cover, and simmer gently for 2–3 hours. Taste and adjust the seasoning to your liking, then garnish with parsley.

BEET SOUP

Serves 4 to 6

1 tablespoon olive oil

2 red onions, chopped

10 beets, cooked, peeled, and diced (see page 56)

4¼ cups (1 liter) good-quality chicken or vegetable stock

2 floury potatoes (approx. 8 oz each), peeled and diced

4 tablespoons chopped fresh chives

Salt and freshly ground black pepper

Heavy cream, to serve

In a large soup pot, heat the oil over medium heat and sauté the onions until soft and translucent. Add the beets, stock, and potatoes, bring to a boil, then reduce the heat to low and simmer gently for 10 minutes, or until the beets are easily pierced with a knife.

Add the chopped chives, reserving some to garnish if you like. Using a blender, food processor, or hand-held immersion blender, purée the soup until smooth. Taste and season to your liking.

Serve with swirl of heavy cream on top.

ROAST TURKEY WITH BACON AND GRAVY

Serves 10 to 14

8–11 lb (4–5 kg) whole organic turkey, neck and giblets removed

5 tablespoons (75 g) butter, softened

4 oz (100 g) bacon

Coarse salt and freshly ground black pepper (adjust to suit your
   taste; I use a little more pepper than salt)

Gravy

Juices from roasting pan

2 onions, peeled and coarsely chopped

1 carrot, coarsely chopped

2–3 bay leaves

Herbs of your preference

2½ cups (600 ml) water

1 tablespoon flour or cornstarch, or more if needed (optional)

Salt and freshly ground black pepper

Preheat the oven to 350°F (180°C). Rinse the turkey under cold running water and pat-dry with paper towels. Rub the butter all over the skin, season generously with salt and freshly ground black pepper, and lay the slices of bacon across the top. Lay it in a large roasting pan, breast side up.

Roast in the center of the oven for 45 minutes per 2 lb (900 g), plus an extra 20 minutes to brown the skin. (E.g., a bird weighing 11 lb/5 kg will take about 4 hours to cook.) If you prefer to wrap your bird in foil, add an extra hour to the cooking time; remove the foil 30 minutes before the end of the cook time to brown the skin.

Baste the bird regularly during the cooking. To test if your turkey is cooked, pierce through the thickest part of the leg as far as you can with a skewer or a sharp knife. When you remove the knife or skewer, check to see if the liquid that comes out is clear. If so, it is ready; if the liquid is the slightest bit red then the bird is not cooked so put it back in the oven until ready. Once cooked, remove it from the oven, cover in foil, and place on a serving platter to rest for 30 minutes before serving.

While the turkey is resting, make the gravy. Strain the juices from the bottom of your roasting pan into a large saucepan and place over medium-high heat. Add the onions, carrots, bay leaves, herbs, and water, season with salt and pepper to your liking, and bring to a boil. Reduce the heat to low and simmer for 20 minutes until thickened. If you like a thicker gravy, strain the liquid through a seive into another saucepan, then whisk in the flour or cornstarch, then simmer over low heat until it reaches your desired consistency.

ROAST CHICKEN

Serves 4 to 6

3 lb (1.5 kg) whole organic chicken
8 tablespoons (115 g) butter, cubed
Olive oil, for drizzling

Preheat the oven to 340°F (170°C). Pat dry with paper towels, then lay the bird on a baking tray. With the head end towards you, lift the skin and press the pieces of butter between the flesh and the skin. Tuck the loose skin back down and drizzle olive oil all over the bird.

Roast in the center of the oven for 1 hour, then turn up the temperature to 375°F (190°C) and roast for an additional 10–20 minutes to brown the skin. To test if your chicken is cooked, pierce through the thickest part of the leg as far as you can with a skewer or a sharp knife. When you remove the knife or skewer, check to see if the liquid that comes out is clear. If so, it is ready; if the liquid is the slightest bit red then the bird is not cooked so put it back in the oven until ready.

When the bird is golden and cooked, remove it from the oven and let it rest for 10 minutes before carving.

VARIATIONS ON ROAST CHICKEN

Chicken with Thyme
Prepare as in the basic Roast Chicken recipe but mix the butter with 1 cup (60 g) fresh thyme (reserving some for sprinkling) before rubbing under the skin. Sprinkle the reserved thyme over the bird before roasting.

Chicken with Honey
Prepare the basic Roast Chicken recipe. Brush the skin with 2 tablespoons of runny honey 10 minutes before the chicken is finished cooking.

Chicken with Garlic
Prepare the basic Roast Chicken recipe but mix the butter with 3–4 crushed garlic cloves before rubbing under the skin.

CHESTNUT STUFFING

Serves 10

1 tablespoon (15 g) butter

2 slices of bacon, diced

1 onion, chopped

2 garlic cloves, finely chopped

12 oz (300 g) sausage meat

3 tablespoons dried breadcrumbs

1 egg, beaten

A pinch of ground nutmeg

8 oz (200 g) cooked, peeled chestnuts, chopped

A good pinch of salt and freshly ground black pepper

(or adjust to suit your taste)

In a large frying pan, melt the butter over medium heat and gently fry the bacon, onion, and garlic until the bacon is crispy. Remove from the heat.

Once the bacon cools slightly, add the sausage, stir thoroughly to make sure the ingredients are well blended, and then add the breadcrumbs and egg. Stir until everything has been combined then add the nutmeg, chopped chestnuts, salt, and pepper. Mix thoroughly then place and cook in the bird, or roast separately, wrapped in foil, at 350°F (180°C) for 1 hour.

VARIATION: For a meat-free chestnut sstuffing, double the amount of chestnuts and replace the sausage with 1 cup (100 g) of chopped, fried mushrooms. Mix in 1 beaten egg to bind it.

CRANBERRY SAUCE

Serves 10

The sour little cranberry, transformed into a sweet sauce, makes the perfect accompaniment to roast turkey or chicken. You could also try Cherry Sauce (page 170) and Redcurrant Jelly (page 171), which go well with white meat and game and can be made from frozen fruit.

> 2 cups (200 g) cranberries
> Generous ⅓ cup (75 g) sugar
> A pinch of ground cinnamon or ground ginger (optional)

Put the cranberries in a large pot, cover with water, and bring to a boil. Cook for 10 minutes, or until soft.

Drain the cranberries. Put them back in the pot over medium heat, add the sugar and cinnamon or ginger, if using, and cook for another 5–10 minutes, stirring and mashing with the back of a spoon occasionally until it forms a thick purée or your desired consistency.

HONEY-ROAST RACK OF PORK

Serves 4

> 3–4 lb (1.5–1.75 kg) rack of pork
> Honey or brown sugar

Place the rack of pork in a large pot with enough water to cover and simmer for 30–45 minutes per 2 lb (900 g).

Preheat the oven to 350°F (180°C). Remove the rack from the water, pat dry, and transfer to a roasting pan. Coat with honey or brown sugar, and roast in the oven until the pork has a crispy brown surface, 10–15 minutes.

ROAST PORK WITH SAGE

Serves 4 to 6

Adapt this basic recipe with any spices of your choosing: Caraway seeds, coriander seeds, cumin, garlic, rosemary, sage, fennel, mustard, savory, and thyme all complement the flavor of pork.

>   4 lb (1.75 kg) pork roast (loin, lean-rolled belly, or boneless shoulder)
>   Olive oil, for drizzling
>   4 fresh sage leaves, or ½ teaspoon dried sage
>   2 heads of garlic, split into cloves but still in their papery skins

Preheat the oven to 325°F (170°C). Put the pork in a roasting tray, drizzle all over with olive oil, and scatter the sage over the top. Lay several garlic cloves over the top and put the rest around the pork. Roast for 2–3 hours. To test if it is cooked, pierce with a sharp knife—if the juices run clear it is done. If you have a meat thermometer, the center of the roast should be 145°F (60°C). Remove from the oven and let it rest for at least 10 minutes before slicing.

ROAST GOOSE

Serves 8 to 10

Goose is the traditional food of the Victorian Christmas table. The goose itself is a remarkable bird, brave (have you ever seen them act as watchdogs on the farm?) and loyal (they mate for life and bring up their goslings in pairs; geese also will look after any wounded members of their gaggles). To me the goose symbolizes fidelity and it also epitomizes the goodness of the "instinct" given to us by mother nature—who we pagans call the Goddess. Give thanks for all the meat on your Yule table and be sure not to waste any.

> 1 leek, coarsely chopped
> 1 apple, quartered
> 1 onion, quartered
> 13 lb (6 kg) goose
> A good pinch of salt and freshly ground black pepper
>   (or adjust to suit your taste)
> Butter or extra goose fat

Preheat oven to 400°F (200°C). Put the leek, apple, and onion inside the goose. Using fine scizzors, make snips all over the skin and fat of the goose and rub in the salt and pepper.

Rub butter or goose fat over the legs of the goose and cover them with foil. Line a large roasting pan with long pieces of foil, both lenthwise and widthwise. Place the goose on a wire rack in the roasting pan and fold the foil over the bird to cover it completely.

Roast for about 3 hours and 45 minutes. After 1 hour, remove the foil, skim the fat from the pan juices (I reserve the fat to use with my Roast Potatoes, page 91) and baste the goose with the juices. Cover with the foil again and return to the oven. Continue to baste every 30 minutes.

For the last 45 minutes, take the foil off to brown the skin. Remove from the oven and stick a metal skewer in the thickest part of the thigh. If the juices run clear, it is ready. If they do not, continue cooking for a little longer until heated through. Leave to rest for at least 10 minutes before carving and serving.

TABBOULEH WITH POMEGRANATE   *Serves 4*

This is my version of tabbouleh, a Middle Eastern dish originally from Syria and Lebanon. The pomegranate is in season in the northern hemisphere from October to February. I always think of pomegranate as a (rather exotic) winter fruit because you start to see lots of them around Halloween time. This is a great pantry dish for me because I always have all of the ingredients in the house—all year—apart from the pomegranate. It brings a little freshness to winter eating.

HOW TO PREPARE A POMEGRANATE

Preparing a pomegranate for cooking or eating is quite simple. Place the whole pomegranate on your work surface and put the palm of your hand on top of it. Pressing firmly, roll the fruit around and around—this will loosen the pomegranate seeds inside. Cut the fruit in half, hold the cut end over a bowl, and, using a wooden spoon or rolling pin, tap the skin hard several times and the seeds will drop into your bowl. If there are any seeds left in the skin, turn the skin inside out and pop out them with a teaspoon. You can now add the pomegranate seeds to any recipe or just eat them!

> Scant 1 cup (180 g) bulgur
> Cold water
> Juice of 3 lemons
> Generous ⅓ cup (90 ml) olive oil
> 3 tomatoes, coarsely chopped
> 1 medium red onion, coarsely chopped
> 4 garlic cloves, chopped
> 1 tablespoon chopped fresh parsley, or 1 teaspoon dried parsley
> 1 tablespoon chopped fresh mint, or 1 teaspoon dried parsley
> Seeds from 1 pomegranate
> Salt and freshly ground black pepper

Place the bulgur in a large bowl, cover with cold water, and leave to soak for 15–20 minutes. Once soaked, pour the bulgur into a sieve and run cold water over it to rinse it, making sure any excess water has drained before using. Transfer to a salad bowl, add the rest of the ingredients, season to taste, and mix thoroughly before serving.

TABBOULEH WITH SMOKED OYSTERS   *Serves 4*

When to eat oysters? The old adage of only when there's an R in the month is kind of true but just for fresh oysters. These ones, however, are preserved, smoked oysters. So this exotic entrée is, again, a pantry recipe of mine. Perfect to bring a bit of zing to your winter menus, which can become a little stew-based at this time of year.

Scant 1 cup (180 g) bulgur
Juice of 3 lemons
Generous ⅓ cup (90 ml) olive oil
3 tomatoes, coarsely chopped
1 medium red onion, coarsely chopped
4 garlic cloves, chopped
1 tablespoon chopped fresh parsley, or 1 teaspoon dried parsley
1 tablespoon chopped fresh mint, or 1 teaspoon dried mint
3 oz (85 g) can smoked oysters
Salt and finely ground black pepper

Place the bulgur in a large bowl, cover with cold water, and leave to soak for 15–20 minutes. Once soaked, pour the bulgur into a sieve and run cold water over it to rinse it, making sure any excess water has drained before using.

Transfer to a salad bowl, add the rest of the ingredients, season to taste, and mix thoroughly before serving.

STAR ANISE CARROTS

Serves 6

These carrots can be cooked in a variety of ways—my preference is to boil, drain, then fry them because I like the nice *jus* that is formed by the butter and honey. If you decide to roast them instead, do not add the honey until the last 10 minutes of cooking time. Star anise has a strong liquorice flavor and would blend well with fennel for ritual or spell work.

> 6 large carrots, peeled and cut into 1-inch (2.5 cm) pieces
> 6 whole star anise
> 4 tablespoons (60 g) butter
> 1 tablespoon honey

Place the carrots in a pot with enough cold water to cover them, add the star anise, and bring to a boil over high heat. Turn the heat down to low and simmer for 10–15 minutes, until they are cooked to your liking.

Drain the carrots and return them to the pot, along with the butter and honey. Warm over low heat for a few minutes until the carrots have been glazed with the honey and a flavorful liquid has formed. Remove the star anise before serving.

COLESLAW DELUXE

Serves 6 to 10

Holiday dinners always need a bit of this—my favorite coleslaw.

> 1 whole white cabbage, damaged leaves and stalk
> removed, leaves finely shredded
> 1 teaspoon sugar
> 1 large carrot, grated
> 1 red onion, finely diced
> 1 tablespoon heavy cream
> 1 tablespoon brandy
> Approx. 1 cup (230 g) Mayonnaise (page 33)

Place the shredded cabbage in a large bowl and stir in the sugar. Add the carrot, onion, and cream and mix, then add the brandy and mix again. Add enough mayonnaise, a tablespoon at a time, until you reach your desired coleslaw consistency. Thoroughly mix the coleslaw and store in the refrigerator for at least 1 hour before serving.

ROAST POTATOES

Serves 4

If you don't have semolina, you can use wheat flour or rice flour, but semolina makes the potatoes crunchier.

> ¾ cup (125 g) semolina
> 4 cloves, crushed
> 2 tablespoons thyme, crushed
> A good pinch of salt and freshly ground black pepper
> (or adjust to suit your taste)
> 3 lb (1.5 kg) potatoes, peeled and cut to your preferred size
> 5 tablespoons olive oil (or goose fat if you have it)
> 1 garlic bulb, split into cloves and peeled

In a bowl, mix together the semolina, cloves, thyme, and salt and pepper and combine thoroughly.

Preheat the oven to 350°F (180°C). Put the potatoes and olive oil (or goose fat) in a large bowl and mix with your hands to completely cover the potatoes with a light coating of the oil. Drain any excess oil then spread them out on a baking sheet. Sprinkle with the semolina mixture and garlic cloves. Roast for 45–60 minutes, or until they are easily pierced with a knife.

STICKY TOFFEE PUDDING

Serves 6

3 oz (90 g) dates or prunes, chopped

Generous ⅓ cup (90 ml) boiling water

½ teaspoon vanilla extract

3 tablespoons (45 g) butter, softened,
    plus extra for greasing

3 tablespoons (45 g) brown sugar

1 egg, beaten

1 teaspoon blackstrap molasses

½ teaspoon baking soda

¾ cup (90 g) self-rising flour

Generous ⅓ cup (90 ml) milk

Whipped cream, crème fraiche, or
    Custard (page 32), to serve

Sauce

2 tablespoons (30 g) butter

Scant ½ cup (90 g) brown sugar

⅔ cup (150 ml) heavy cream

1 tablespoon blackstrap molasses

Preheat the oven to 350°F (180°C). Place the dates or prunes in a bowl, cover with the boiling water, add the vanilla, and set aside to soak for 5 minutes.

Using an electric hand mixer or stand mixer, cream together the butter and brown sugar. Add the egg and molasses and mix thoroughly. Fold in the baking soda, about one-third of the flour, and half of the milk until incorporated; repeat until all the milk and flour have been incorporated. Drain and mash the dried fruit and add them to the mixing bowl.

Grease six small ramekins (about 5 oz/150 ml capacity) with butter, then fill them with the mixture. Bake for 20–25 minutes, or until a toothpick inserted into the center comes out clean.

Meanwhile, make the sauce: Melt the butter, sugar, and half the cream in a small saucepan and bring to a boil over low heat. Simmer, stirring, for 5 minutes, until the sugar has dissolved. Stir in the molasses, turn up the heat to medium, and simmer for another 2–3 minutes until a rich toffee color. Remove from the heat and beat in the rest of the cream.

Carefully turn each of the puddings out onto serving plates and pour the sauce over the tops. Serve with a dollop of whipped cream, crème fraiche, or custard.

CLOOTIE DUMPLING

Serves 6

1⅔ cups (200 g) self-rising flour, sifted,
    plus extra for dusting

1 cup (100 g) breadcrumbs or rolled oats

½ teaspoon salt

1 teaspoon baking powder

Generous ⅓ cup (75 g) brown sugar

1 tablespoon golden syrup

7 tablespoons (100 g) vegetable
    shortening or beef suet, or grated
    frozen butter

⅔ cup (100 g) raisins

⅔ cup (100 g) golden raisins

Chopped or grated zest of 1 orange, or
    1½ oz (50 g) mixed candied peel

1 apple, grated

1 heaped teaspoon cinnamon

1 heaped teaspoon ground ginger

1 heaped teaspoon allspice

1 teaspoon grated nutmeg

2 eggs

Approx. 1 cup (240 ml) milk

Boiling water

To serve (optional)

Custard (page 32)

Brandy butter

Whipped cream

Butter

In a large mixing bowl, combine all the ingredients, except the milk and boiling water. Gently mix, then pour in enough milk to form a very wet dough.

Quickly scald a large cheesecloth with boiling water and then spread it out and dust the center with flour. Spoon the mixture into the center and tie it up, leaving a little room for the mixture to swell.

Place an inverted heatsafe plate in the bottom of a large soup pot and place the bundle on top. Fill the pot with boiling water, cover, and boil for 4–5 hours. Keep an eye on it—do not let the pot run out of water. It is ready when it feels firm and solid (not soft and spongy).

Serve hot with custard, brandy butter, or whipped cream, or cold spread with butter.

APRICOT TART

Serves 4 to 6

1 cup (190 g) dried apricots

6 tablespoons (90 g) butter, plus extra for greasing

1⅔ cups (180 g) self-rising flour

Scant 1 cup (180 g) brown sugar

A pinch of salt

2 eggs

½ teaspoon vanilla extract

A handful of nuts (almonds or hazelnuts work well), chopped

2 tablespoons granulated sugar

Confectioners' sugar, for dusting (optional)

Place the apricots in a saucepan over high heat, cover with cold water, and bring to a boil. Reduce the heat to low and simmer for 10 minutes. Rinse them in cold water, drain, then leave to cool.

Preheat the oven to 350°F (180°C) and lightly grease a 9-inch (23 cm) springform cake pan (or use a nonstick cake pan). In a mixing bowl, add the butter, half the flour, and half the brown sugar then mix with your fingers until it resembles fine breadcrumbs. Press the mixture firmly into the bottom of the pan and bake for 10 to 12 minutes, or until golden.

Remove the pan from the oven and set aside (but do not remove the base from the pan). Turn down the oven to 300°F (150°C).

In another mixing bowl, combine the remaining flour, brown sugar, salt, and eggs and mix well. Add the vanilla extract, nuts, and boiled apricots and stir through.

Spread this mixture over the base, sprinkle with the granulated sugar, and bake for 30 minutes. Leave the tart to cool before removing from the pan. The tart can be sliced and served undecorated or it can be dusted with confectioners' sugar.

SPICED TEA

Serves 1

4 whole cloves
A pinch of ground ginger
A pinch of ground allspice
A pinch of ground cinnamon
A pinch of ground nutmeg
Generous 1½ cups (375 ml) water
1 teaspoon English breakfast tea leaves
Honey or sugar, to serve (optional)

In a small saucepan, combine all of the spices and the water. Bring to a boil over medium-high heat, then turn off the heat, add the tea leaves, and let stand for 3–5 minutes to steep. Pour into a mug and sweeten with honey or sugar to taste.

SPICED MILK

Serves 1

A pinch of ground ginger, plus extra to serve
A pinch of ground allspice
A pinch of ground cinnamon, plus extra to serve
A pinch of ground nutmeg
Sugar, to taste
Generous 1½ cups (375 ml) milk

In a small saucepan, combine all of the ingredients together. Bring to a boil over medium-high heat, without letting the milk burn, then turn the heat down to low and simmer gently for 5 minutes. Pour into a mug and add another pinch of ginger or cinnamon (your preference) to the top.

WASSAIL

Makes approx. 2 quarts (2 liters)

Wassail! wassail! all over the town,
Our toast it is white and our ale it is brown;
Our bowl it is made of the white maple tree;
With the wassailing bowl, we'll drink to thee.
—The Gloucestershire Wassail

The word is from Anglo-Saxon *"waes hael,"* a toast meaning "good health," and in the Middle Ages, people drank this hot alcoholic drink at big gatherings, like to see in the New Year. Toasted bread ("sops") would be served on top. This version is lovely ladled into clear punch cups and garnished with lemon wedges. You can vary the spices and amounts of alcohol to suit your taste. You don't need to sing the song, though it is encouraged!

> 3 red apples, halved and deseeded
> 4 tablespoons (60 g) butter
> Grated zest of 1 lemon
> Scant ½ cup (90 g) brown sugar
> A good pinch of cinnamon
> A good pinch of ground ginger
> 4¼ cups (1 liter) sweet stout or beer
> 1¼ cups (300 ml) dry sherry or dry white wine (sherry will be sweeter)
> 2 cups (480 ml) brandy
> Lemon wedges, to serve (optional)

In a large pot, slowly melt the butter over low heat, add the apples, lemon zest, sugar, and spices, and cook gently for 5 minutes.

Add the beer, wine, and brandy to the pot, turn up the heat to medium, and heat to just before boiling. Reduce the heat to low and simmer for 30 minutes. Serve hot with lemon wedges.

If you are not serving it immediately, leave it to cool completely before storing in the refrigerator. When you are ready to serve your wassail, return it to low heat to warm through.

IMBOLC

I light these candles to clean and to heal.
Let flame light my purpose—let candle reveal
The good work I've done—and the work that remains.
I give thanks for our house and for all it contains.
Let body and mind and home be cleansed.
An it harm none so be it.

CHAPTER FOUR

IMBOLC

OR CANDLEMAS (FEBRUARY 2ND)

On the day of the February festival of Imbolc (or St. Brigid's day), pagans celebrate the recovery of the Goddess Brighid (or Brigid) who is renewed as the maiden after the birth of the God. Brighid is one of the many goddesses of hearth and home. Her symbol is the hearth or stove.

Imbolc marks the beginning of spring. In ancient times, tribes, clans, and villages would gather together to honor the Celtic Goddess, Bride, or Brighid (later Christianized as St. Brigid) and ask for healing for the sick following a harsh winter. The word "Imbolc" means "in the belly" referring to the bulbs and seeds lying in the earth, perhaps dropped by the birds the previous year, waiting for the right time to sprout. Imbolc is also when calves and lambs are born and cows and sheep produce milk for their young. For this reason, milk and dairy products are popular among pagans at this time. The young God is growing in strength and the Goddess is growing more beautiful with each passing day.

IMBOLC COLORS

The colors associated with Imbolc are white, pink, red, yellow, green, and brown.

IMBOLC CRYSTALS

Crystals associated with Imbolc are amethyst, rose quartz, citrine, tiger's eye, and bloodstone.

IMBOLC INCENSE

Incense can be made using dried basil, bay, wisteria, cinnamon, violet, vanilla, and myrrh oil. To any of these base ingredients you can add various gums or resins, such as gum Arabic or myrrh resin. Put your mixture into a small jar and label accordingly. This mixture can be sprinkled over charcoal disks.

IMBOLC PURPOSE

Carry out rituals for healing and fertility at this time. Fertility on this occasion relates to the earth, so this is a good time to bless the seeds that will be planted to ensure a good crop. Farmers need their animals to produce healthy young so we must remember to include these wishes in our rituals. Healing spells can also relate to healing the planet and countries at war or in conflict. Imbolc is a time of purification, which makes it a good time to think about cleansing—mentally, spiritually, and physically. All spring cleaning should be done now and we begin by cleaning the house from top to bottom. Strip back the beds and let the mattresses air by leaving the windows open. You can make up a cleaning mixture from the cleaning recipes shown on pages 247–248.

When all your cleaning is done you can celebrate the arrival of Imbolc, a festival of light, by lighting perfumed candles in every room. Let your candles burn for as long as possible but be sure to do this safely.

> *I light these candles to clean and to heal*
> *Let flame light my purpose—let candle reveal*
> *The good work that I've done—and the work that remains.*
> *I give thanks for our house and for all it contains.*
> *Let body and mind and home be cleansed*
> *An it harm none so be it.*

IMBOLC SELF-DEDICATION RITE

Imbolc is a perfect time to perform a self-dedication and to renew your promise to the God and Goddess. Or, if you are just starting out in Wicca, and since you have cleaned your home from top to bottom, now would be a very good time to welcome them into your life. As with all rituals or ceremonies in the following pages, please feel free to amend the words to suit your own needs, preferences, or purposes.

Please refer to the instructions on page 41 (Samhain Ritual) to set up your circle. Then say these words or create your own:

> *The circle is about to be cast.*
> *Let none be here but of their own free will.*

Pick up your matches and move to the east and light the east candle saying:

Here do I bring into the east light and air to illuminate this circle and bring it the breath of life.

The south candle is lit saying:

Here do I bring into the south light and fire to illuminate this circle and bring it warmth.

The west candle is lit saying:

Here do I bring into the west light and water to illuminate this circle and wash it clean.

The north candle is lit saying:

Here do I bring into the north light and earth to illuminate this circle and build it in strength.

Return to your altar and say:

This circle line I now prepare,
Let no one enter should they dare.
This sacred space I dedicate,
Filled with love and never hate.
So mote it be.

Pick up your athame or wand or use the index finger of your dominant hand to draw a circle in the air, starting at the east, reaching the south, the west, then the north, and back to the east. Next touch the salt on your altar with your athame, wand, or index finger and say:

As salt is life, let it purify me so that I may use it to cleanse my body and spirit in honor of the God and Goddess.

Put three pinches of salt in the water dish then raise your hand high pointing your athame, wand, or index finger upwards, feeling the energy flowing into your arm. Put your athame, wand, or index finger into the water and stir three times, saying:

Salt is life, here is life, blessed be without strife, salt is life, here is life, blessed be without strife, salt is life, here is life, sacred be without strife.

Sprinkle the salted water around the circle edge starting at the east, moving to the south, the west, then the north, and back to the east. Return to your altar and put down the consecrated water. Light any altar candles and your incense, then pick up the athame or wand or use your index finger to call the elemental guardians by drawing pentacles in the air saying:

With air, fire, water, and earth, I purify and charge you, east, hail guardians of the watchtower of the east, I invoke you [insert the name of the God or Goddess of your choice], come by the air that is your breath, may you stand in strength ever watching over this circle.

With fire, water, earth, and air, I purify and charge you, south, hail guardians of the watchtower of the south, I invoke you [insert the name of the God or Goddess of your choice], come by the fire that is your spirit, may you stand in strength ever watching over this circle.

With water, earth, air, and fire, I purify and charge you, west, hail guardians of the watchtower of the west, I invoke you [insert the name of the God or Goddess of your choice], come by the waters of your earthy womb that give us life, may you stand in strength ever watching over this circle.

With earth, air, fire, and water, I purify and charge you, north, hail guardians of the watchtower of the north, I invoke you [insert the name of the God or Goddess of your choice], come by the earth that is your body, may you stand in strength ever watching over this circle.

Take a drink from the chalice and focus your mind on the God and the Goddess. Then, standing in the Goddess position with your arms held high, invoke the Goddess energy into yourself and say:

Lady you have been known by many. I worship and adore you and invite you to join me in body and spirit. Be with me and guide me in the true ways.

Pick up your athame or wand or use your index finger and draw a pentacle in the air above you and below you and say:

You are here and I thank you for the gifts that you have given. I know that you only help those who help themselves. I ask:

By candlelight I make my vow,
The Old Ways fore'er from now.
I name myself [your craft name] in the witches' way,
This I be known as from this day.
It is my will for all to see,
Let it harm none, so mote it be.

Before the God and Goddess, from this moment on, I [your name] will be known as [your craft name] within the circle of the wise, to symbolize my rebirth.

I promise to honor the God and the Goddess in all areas of my life. I will work to understand
their great mysteries.
I will work to understand the mystery of myself.
I will share my knowledge with those who seek my help.
I will protect and guard the Old Ways from those who would scorn them.
I will defend the God and Goddess.
I will work in harmony with the earth.
I will honor plant, animal, spirit, and man.
I will embrace the elements of air, fire, water, and earth.
I will honor and respect my brothers and sisters within or outwith the craft.
An it harm none do what thou will.
What we send forth will return thrice over, so we send it forth with light and love.
So mote it be.

Visualize your prayers and wishes rising to the moon Goddess. Pick up the chalice or cup in your
left hand and the athame or wand in your right hand and hold them at eye level then place the
point of the athame or wand or your index finger into the wine and say:

May male and female be joined and let all be fruitful throughout the land. The food I eat is
the blessing of the Gods and I remember those who have none. I am grateful for all I have
been given and am open and ready to receive that which is still to come, so mote it be.
We have met in love and friendship, let us part the same way, spreading the love from this
circle outward to all, sharing it with those we meet. Lord and Lady my thanks to you for
sharing this time with me, guarding and guiding me.
Merry we meet, merry we part, merry we meet again.
The circle will now be closed.

Finish with:

Take for your use, eastern watchtower, any powers of air that have not been used.
Take for your use, southern watchtower, any powers of fire that have not been used.
Take for your use, western watchtower, any powers of water that have not been used.
Take for your use, northern watchtower, any powers of earth that have not been used.

The circle is now closed but the work continues.
Let it harm none, so mote it be.

IMBOLC FOODS

All foods containing yogurt, cheese, eggs, butter, milk, dried fruits, honey, raisins, onions, leeks, shallots, garlic, saffron, turmeric. Curries, spiced wines, and spiced teas are appropriate too. Things that evoke the hearth, such as breads, bannocks, oatcakes, and griddle scones.

IMBOLC RECIPES

CURD CHEESE

Makes 2–3 pint-size (450 g) jars

This is a great way to use up excess milk and is the easiest cheese to make, without the need for rennet or a starter culture. It is very mild tasting with a small curd, a bit like ricotta in consistency. You can add sweet or savory flavors to it; see the Variations at the end for my suggestions.

Cheese
1 quart (1 liter) milk
2 tablespoons lemon juice or white vinegar
¼ teaspoon salt
Olive oil, for greasing your hands

Garlic Marinade
Olive oil, for filling the jars
4 garlic cloves, whole, per jar
Salt and freshly ground black pepper

A jelly bag or a clean cheesecloth
2–3 pint-size (450 g) jars with lids, sterilized (see page 57)
A digital thermometer

Scald a large soup pot with boiling water and ensure all the utensils you are using are scalded and very clean. Drain all water from the pot and add the milk. Gently heat on the lowest heat setting until it is just below boiling point—190°F (80°C). Add the lemon juice, a tablespoon at a time, until the milk curdles, then add the salt, mix a little, and set aside to cool.

When cool, pour it into a jelly bag or cheesecloth-lined colander set over a bowl. Gather together the ends, tie it up, and hang it over an empty container. Leave it in a cool place to drain overnight.

The next day, it should resemble a crumbly cheese. Now the fun part: divid the cheese into sections. Rub olive oil over your hands and divide and roll the cheese into 1½-inch (4 cm) balls. Drop the balls into one of your empty sterilized jars until the jar is half full. Add the garlic cloves and fill the jar to about 1 inch (2.5 cm) from the top with olive oil, making sure that the cheese is completely covered. Add salt and pepper to taste and gently mix. Put the lid on tightly and store in the refrigerator. Repeat until all the cheese is used up. This is fabulous as an appetizer with crusty bread and olives.

This will keep for a few days stored in the refrigerator, but I can't tell you exactly how long because it never lasts long enough in our house!

VARIATIONS: As an alternative to the garlic, you can add your favorite herbs such as saffron, turmeric, chives, bay leaves, or basil before filling the jar with olive oil to about an inch from the top, making sure that the cheese is completely covered.

If you want a cottage-cheese type curd, drain the curds but do not leave them overnight in the cheesecloth or jelly bag. You can add a little cream to the curds to make it smooth like store-bought cottage cheese. If you want an Indian paneer-type cheese, after draining away the liquid, tie the cheesecloth tightly, put a weight on top, and leave overnight but do not marinate.

POTATO AND LEEK SOUP

Serves 4 to 6

3 lb (1.5 kg) potatoes, peeled
8½ cups (2 liters) ham stock (page 25)
2 large leeks (with green parts)
Salt and freshly ground black pepper
Cream, to serve
Freshly grated nutmeg, to serve

Put the potatoes and stock in a large stockpot over low heat while you prepare the leeks.

Cut the root from each leek and cut again where the white meets the green. Cut the white parts lengthwise, cut in half, then roughly dice. Place them in a colander in the sink under cold running water for a minute to clean them, then add them to the pot. Roughly dice the green parts of the leeks, then place them in the colander under cold running tap water to clean them for a minute. Add the green pieces to the pot.

Increase the heat to high and bring the soup to a boil. Lower the heat and simmer for 20 minutes, or until the potatoes start to break up.

Turn off the heat and set aside to cool. Once the soup is cooled, use a blender, food processor, or hand-held immersion blender to blend to a creamy consistency. Return the soup to the pot over low heat and season to taste before serving. Top each bowl with a drizzle of cream and a grating of fresh nutmeg.

LAMB STEW

2 lb (950g) lamb chops

3¾ cups (900 ml) water

2 medium onions, coarsely chopped

4 carrots, sliced

4 potatoes, thickly sliced

A good pinch of parsley

1 teaspoon fresh chives, chopped, or a good pinch of dried chives

1 teaspoon flour or cornstarch, or more if needed (optional)

A good pinch of salt and freshly ground black pepper

    (or adjust to suit your taste)

Preheat the oven to 425°F (220°C). Cut the fat and bones from the lamb chops, place the fat and bones in a roasting pan, and roast in the oven for 30 minutes, or until the fat is rendered. Discard the bones and transfer the rendered fat to a Dutch oven.

Lower the oven temperature to 350°F (180°C). Put the lamb chops in the hot fat and add the water, vegetables, herbs, salt and pepper. Cover and braise for 1½–2 hours (the meat should be nice and tender). If there is too much fat at the end of the cooking time, lay a slice of dry bread on top to soak up excess.

If you would like a thicker stew, strain the liquid into a saucepan and set it over low heat. Whisk in the flour or cornstarch and simmer for 5–10 minutes until the mixture reaches your desired consistency, then return it to the pot. Serve with boiled baby potatoes and green vegetables.

BACON AND ONION QUICHE

Serves 4 to 6

If you have eggs, flour, and butter on hand, you can always whip up a quiche for any unexpected visitors! This one contains bacon and onions, but you can use broccoli, cheese, mushrooms, tomatoes, herbs, or any combination of these you like, or to suit what you have on hand.

> 1 portion Shortcrust Pastry (page 28)
> 4 eggs
> 1 tablespoon milk
> 1 onion, finely chopped
> 2–3 slices of cooked bacon, diced
> 4 slices of raw bacon
> Salt and freshly ground black pepper

Preheat the oven to 400°F (200°C). Roll out the pastry to a round a littlle bigger than 8 inches (20 cm) in diameter and ¼ inch (0.5 cm) thick. Use it to line an 8-inch (20 cm) pie dish or flan pan then trim off any ends.

In a bowl, whisk the eggs and milk together. Add the onion, cooked bacon, and salt and pepper to taste. Pour this mixture into your pie dish and lay the slices of raw bacon in a crisscross pattern across the top.

Bake the quiche for 30 minutes, or until the egg has puffed up and the bacon on top is crispy. It can be served hot or cold.

SPICY OMELET

Serves 2 to 3

If you have eggs in your refrigerator, you always have the potential for a fine meal. You can add chopped peppers, onions, or anything else that takes your fancy to this omelet too. If you add other ingredients, put them into the frying pan first to heat through before adding the eggs. This might be a bit spicy for some people at breakfast time, so you could serve it for lunch, along with Breakfast Tomatoes (next page) or Mexican Potato Salad (page 114) if you like.

> 4 tablespoons (60 g) butter
> 3 large eggs
> A good pinch of curry powder
> A good pinch of cayenne
> 1 teaspoon water
> A pinch of salt and freshly ground black pepper
>> (or adjust to suit your taste)

Melt the butter in a nonstick frying pan over medium-high heat. Break the eggs into a bowl and add the spices, water, and seasoning. Beat (but not too much) and add them to the frying pan. Leave for a moment until the sides set then pull the sides away from the pan using a palette knife or spatula and let the raw eggs flow into the gaps. Repeat this process until all the eggs have set (this should take no more than a minute or two).

BREAKFAST TOMATOES WITH EGGS   *Serves 2 to 3*

1 tablespoon olive oil

1 onion, finely chopped

3 garlic cloves, finely chopped

8 tomatoes, skinned, cored, and chopped

A good pinch of fresh oregano

1 tablespoon tomato paste

4 eggs

Salt and freshly ground black pepper

Buttered toast, to serve (optional)

Warm the olive oil in a large skillet that has a lid (preferably transparent) over low heat. Add the onion and garlic and cook until the onion is transluscent. Add the tomatoes and thoroughly mix. Add the oregano, stir again, cover with the lid, and cook for 10 minutes.

Add the tomato paste, stir well, cover with the lid, and cook for a further 10 minutes. The mixture should be thick and stay in place—if it flows too quickly when stirred, leave the lid off and reduce it for a few more minutes.

Remove the lid and, using a spoon, push the mixture away from the side of the pan. Break an egg into the space. Repeat this process with each egg then put the lid on and poach the eggs in the tomato mixture.

Season to taste and serve with buttered toast.

NOTES: To skin tomatoes, pierce them with a sharp knife and drop them into a bowl of boiling water for a few minutes—the skin will then peel off easily.

MACARONI AND CHEESE

Serves 2 to 4

1 teaspoon salt

4 oz (120 g) dry macaroni

4 tablespoons (60 g) butter

½ cup (60 g) all-purpose flour

2½ cups (600 ml) milk

3–4 oz (90–125 g) cheddar cheese (or your favorite kind)

1 teaspoon mustard powder

Topping

¾ cup (60 g) cheddar cheese (or your favorite kind)

Sliced tomatoes

Scant ½ cup (60 g) fresh breadcrumbs

Fill a medium pot with water, add the salt, and bring to a boil. Once the water is boiling, add the macaroni and cook until "al dente" (tender but still with a bite to it) according to the instructions on the package.

As the pasta is cooking, melt the butter in a separate saucepan, add the flour, and cook, stirring, for a few minutes until you have a golden paste. Remove the pan from the heat and briskly stir in a little of the milk. Continue mixing in the milk a little at a time (to avoid lumps forming) until you have a nice thick sauce. Add the cheese and mustard powder and stir until the cheese has melted.

Preheat the oven to 350°F (180°C). When the macaroni is cooked, drain it and place it in a casserole dish. Pour in the cheese sauce and stir well. Sprinkle the grated cheese over the top, garnish with the tomatoes, and then sprinkle with the breadcrumbs. Bake for 10–15 minutes, or until the cheese has melted and the breadcrumbs have turned golden brown.

VARIATION: Chunks of crispy bacon, diced peppers, chopped onions, diced mushrooms, or any combination of the above can be added at the same time as the cheese sauce.

CAULIFLOWER SALAD

Serves 4

Growing up, I always came home from school at lunchtime and this was my favorite dish! It is easy to make and even easier to eat. It is best served chilled with dry crusty bread to dip into the juices that form in the bottom of the bowl. Whenever I serve this, we argue over who gets the most juice!

> 1 large cauliflower, cut into florets (be sure to
>   add the stem and trimmings to your compost heap)
> Juice from 1 lemon and an equal quantity of olive oil,
>   plus extra for serving
> Salt and freshly ground black pepper
> Crusty bread, to serve

Put the cauliflower in a large soup pot, cover with water, and bring to a boil. Reduce the heat to low and simmer for 20 minutes, or until the cauliflower is easily pierced with a knife. Drain and set aside to cool completely.

Put the cauliflower in a large bowl, add the lemon juice and olive oil, and season to taste. Stir thoroughly and leave in the refrigerator for at least 2 hours or overnight. Serve with crusty bread drizzled with extra olive oil and another squeeze of lemon juice.

MEXICAN POTATO SALAD

Serves 4 to 6

3–4 lb (1.5–1.75 kg) potatoes, peeled and quartered
4 slices of bacon, chopped
3 garlic cloves, finely chopped
1 small onion, finely chopped
1 bell pepper (red, yellow, or green), finely diced
1 small zucchini, finely diced
Approx. 1 cup (230 g) Mayonnaise (page 33)
Salt and freshly ground black pepper

Put the potatoes in a soup pot, cover with water, bring to a boil, and cook for 20 minutes, or until they are easily pierced with a knife.

While the potatoes are cooking, fry the bacon pieces until crispy.

Drain the potatoes and transfer to a large bowl. While the potatoes are still hot, add the fried bacon, garlic, onion, bell pepper, and zucchini. Stir in the mayonnaise, one tablespoon at a time, until you reach your desired consistency. Season to taste and serve while it is still warm. Alternatively, you can store the salad in the refrigerator until needed and serve cold.

VINDALOO

Serves 6 to 8

This is a very hot curry and not for the faint-hearted! It is a good base for any meats or vegetables of your choice. It is also a great accompaniment for empowering any spell or banishing ritual.

Part One

4½ lb (2 kg) pork, beef, chicken,
    or lamb, diced
1 cup (240 ml) malt or wine vinegar

Part Two

1 teaspoon cardamom seeds
1 tablespoon ground cayenne
4 cinnamon sticks, each 3 inches
    (7.5 cm) long
12 cloves, whole
1 tablespoon coriander seeds
2 teaspoons fenugreek seeds
1 teaspoon black peppercorns, whole
2 teaspoons salt

2 teaspoons mustard powder
2 teaspoons fresh ginger, minced
2 teaspoons turmeric powder

Part Three

4–6 tablespoons mustard oil or ghee
    (clarified butter), for frying
2 teaspoons cumin seeds
2 teaspoons garlic, minced
2 small onions, diced
1¼ cups (300 ml) water
4 bay leaves
Perfect Rice, to serve (page 35, made
    from 1–2 cups/200–400 g rice)

Part One

Place the meat and vinegar in non-metallic bowl. Mix well and leave to marinate in the refrigerator for 24 hours, turning occasionally.

Part Two

When the meat has been marinated, drain off the vinegar and set aside. In a frying pan, gently dry-roast the cardamom seeds, cayenne, cinnamon, cloves, coriander, fenugreek, and black peppercorns over low heat for 5 minutes. Put them into a blender or food processor and blend together with the salt, mustard powder, ginger, turmeric, and the reserved vinegar to make a paste. If it is a little too dry, add 1 teaspoon of water at a time, blending after each addition, until it reaches your desired consistency.

Part Three

Heat 1–2 tablepoons of the mustard oil or ghee in a frying pan over medium-high heat and fry the cumin, garlic, and onions until the onions are soft. Take off the heat and set aside.

Heat 3–4 tablespoons of the oil or ghee in a large deep pan and fry the meat over high heat for 5 minutes, adding more oil or ghee as needed. Add the spice paste and the onion mixture to the meat, along with the water and the bay leaves, and simmer over medium heat for 1 hour, or until the meat is tender. Taste and add more salt or chili if necessary.

This is best served the next day because it gives the spices a chance to flavor the meat. Serve with Perfect Rice.

CAULIFLOWER WITH CHEESE

Serves 4

1 large cauliflower, cut into florets (be sure to add the stem and
   trimmings to your compost heap)
4 tablespoons (60 g) butter
½ cup (60 g) all-purpose flour
Approx. 2 cups (480 ml) milk
1 teaspoon mustard (any kind)
4 oz (125 g) cheddar cheese (or your favorite kind)
Salt and freshly ground black pepper
Breadcrumbs, for topping

Place the cauliflower in a soup pot, cover with cold water and bring to a boil. Reduce the heat to low, cover, and simmer for 20 minutes, or until the florets can be easily pierced with a knife.

While the cauliflower is cooking, melt the butter in a saucepan. Add the flour and stir constantly for a few minutes until it forms a golden paste. Remove the pan from the heat and briskly stir in a little milk. Continue to add the milk, a little at a time, stirring constantly, until you have a nice thick sauce (any lumps can be stirred out so do not worry if some form). Once you have your desired sauce consistency, add the mustard, salt and pepper to taste, and most of the cheese, reserving a little for the topping. Stir the cheese through the sauce until melted.

Preheat the broiler. Drain the cauliflower and place it in a casserole dish. Pour over the cheese sauce, and give it all a stir. Sprinkle the top with breadcrumbs and the reserved cheese, and place it under the broiler until the breadcrumbs are brown and the cheese has melted. Serve immediately.

SPICY LOAF

Makes 1 small loaf

6 tablespoons (90 g) butter, plus extra for greasing

½ cup (125 ml) golden or maple syrup

1⅔ cups (180 g) self-rising flour

⅔ cup, lightly packed (90 g) dark brown sugar

⅔ cup (125 g) dried fruit

A good pinch of ground ginger

1 teaspoon cinnamon

1 teaspoon freshly grated nutmeg

1 tablespoon poppyseeds

1 egg, beaten

4 tablespoons milk

Preheat the oven to 325°F (160°C). Grease a 2-lb (900 g) loaf pan.

In a small nonstick frying pan, slowly melt the butter and syrup over low heat for 5 minutes.

In a mixing bowl, combine the flour, sugar, dried fruit, ginger, cinnamon, nutmeg, and poppyseeds and stir. Make a well in the middle then pour in the warm liquid. Add the egg and milk and mix well. Pour the dough into the prepared pan and bake for 30–40 minutes, or until the top is golden.

SPELL CAKE

Serves 4 to 6

A plain, but far from bland, cake that is just waiting for your own signature take on it. Decorate and flavor according to your spell work or ritual. At Imbolc, why not add a pinch of saffron, replace some of the sugar with honey, and say:

Let those who share this cake
Enjoy its taste,
Enjoy our company,
Enjoy good health,
And return to us soon,
An it harm none so be it.

9 tablespoons (125 g) butter, plus extra for greasing
Scant 1 cup (180 g) sugar
1 egg, separated
¼–⅓ cup (60–90 ml) water
1⅔ cups (180 g) self-rising flour
Crystalized Petals (page 163), to decorate (optional)

Preheat the oven to 300°F (150°C) and grease an 8-inch (20 cm) round or square cake pan.

In a bowl, use an electric hand mixer or whisk to beat together the butter and sugar until fluffy. Mix in the egg yolk and alternate spoonfuls of water and flour to make a thick but smooth batter.

In a seperate bowl, use an electric hand mixer or whisk to beat the egg white until stiff, then carefully fold into the cake batter.

Pour the batter into the pan and bake for 25 minutes (do not open the oven until you can smell the cake). Test the cake by inserting a skewer into the center—if it comes out clean, it is ready. You can decorate the top with a few Crystalized Petals.

CRESCENT CAKES

Makes approx. 12

1⅔ cups (180 g) self-rising flour
Scant ⅔ cups (125 g) sugar
Scant 1¼ cups (125 g) ground almonds
9 tablespoons (125 g) butter, plus extra for greasing
1 tablespoon honey
1 egg

In a mixing bowl, combine the flour, sugar, and almonds and mix. Add the butter and rub in using your fingers until it resembles fine breadcrumbs. Then add the honey and egg and mix well with a wooden spoon or spatula until you have a firm dough. Cover the bowl with a clean cloth and chill in the refrigerator until cool and firm.

Preheat the oven to 350°F (180°C) and grease a baking sheet. Remove the dough from the refrigerator and roll out until it is ½ inch (2.5 cm) thick. Use a 2½-inch (6 cm) round cutter to cut out circles, then use the same cutter to cut out a part of each circle to form crescents. Re-roll and repeat until you have used all the dough. Space out on the greased baking sheet and bake for 20 minutes, or until golden.

FRUIT AND NUT CAKE

Serves 4 to 6

Scant 1 cup (180 g) sugar
½ cup (125 ml) corn oil
⅔ cup (125 g) dried fruits
1⅔ cups (180 g) self-rising flour
2 eggs
1 cup (125 g) walnuts, chopped
Butter or vegetable oil, for greasing

Preheat the oven to 350°F (180°C) and grease an 8-inch (20 cm) round or square cake pan. Thoroughly mix together the sugar, oil, dried fruits, flour, and eggs until you have a batter. Gently stir in the walnuts. Pour the batter into the cake pan and bake for 20–30 minutes, or until a skewer inserted into the middle of the cake comes out clean. Allow to cool before serving.

NECTAR

Serves 1

This hot drink is made with mead, an alcoholic beverage produced from fermented honey-water. Traditionally, mead contained herbs and spices with ritualistic and spiritual significance for the Celts of the British isles, the Anglo-Saxons, and the Vikings. Mead is available to buy or you can make your own (see page 194), or why not use my Litha Mead (page 192), which is non-alcoholic.

> 1 cup (240 ml) milk
> 3 tablespoons mead
> ½ teaspoon vanilla extract
> 1 teaspoon honey
> A pinch of cinnamon, to serve

Place the milk and mead in a saucepan set over low heat. Add the vanilla extract and honey. Heat through but make sure it does not boil. Sprinkle with cinnamon before serving.

SODA BREAD

Makes 1 loaf

> 1⅔ cups (200 g) all-purpose flour, plus extra for dusting
> 1 teaspoon baking soda
> 2 teaspoons cream of tartar
> 1 teaspoon salt
> ½ cup (125 ml) milk
> Butter or vegetable oil, for greasing

Preheat the oven to 375°F (190°C) and grease and flour a baking sheet. Sift all the dry ingredients together into a bowl. Add the milk and mix with a knife until you have a moist, elastic dough. Flour your work surface and hands and shape the dough into a round, then place it on the baking sheet. Make two slashes on top with a sharp knife to form a cross. Bake for 30–40 minutes, or until nicely browned on top and the bottom sounds hollow when tapped.

GRIDDLE SCONES

Serves 8

1⅔ cups (200 g) all-purpose flour, plus extra for dusting

1 teaspoon baking soda

2 teaspoons cream of tartar

1 teaspoon salt

½ cup (125 ml) milk

2 tablespoons (25 g) melted butter, or more if needed, for greasing

Butter and jam (any kind), to serve

Sift all the dry ingredients together into a bowl, add the milk, and mix with a knife until you have a light, elastic dough (I know it is right when it is almost, but not quite, sticky).

Place a griddle or heavy-based, nonstick frying pan, over medium-high heat.

Divide the dough into two even pieces. On a floured work surface, poll out each piece into a round with a thickness of 1½ inches (4 cm). Cut each circle into four wedges. Grease the hot griddle or pan with the melted butter and cook the wedges for 3–4 minutes per side until golden. Let them cool, wrapped in a tea towel, and serve with butter and jam.

OSTARA

I plant my seed that it may grow,
My hopes within it, too, I sow.
Dear Goddess see what I pursue,
And help me see my dreams come true.
If I deserve it, through work and toil—
Here symbolized by fertile soil—
The day will come, through my volition,
When I will see my work's fruition.
An it harm none so be it.

CHAPTER FIVE

OSTARA

(EASTER)

Traditionally, Easter falls on the first Sunday after the first full moon after the Spring Equinox. At this time, children decorate and roll boiled eggs and receive gifts of chocolate.

For Christians the rolling of eggs is symbolic of rolling away the stone in front of the cave where Christ's body was laid to rest. Pagans have a different slant on this. The Sun God has been growing to maturity while the Goddess has been growing younger and more beautiful. At this point they reach the same age and embrace in love and harmony with each other and conceive the child who will become the God reborn at Yule.

We pagans recognize the egg as a symbol of life and growth and we celebrate the renewal and rebirth of nature and the coming of summer. During Imbolc we had the ideas and made the plans, and Ostara is the time to sow the seeds that were blessed at Imbolc.

OSTARA COLORS

Colors associated with Ostara are lemon-yellow and all pastel colors.

OSTARA CRYSTALS

Crystals associated with Ostara are aquamarine, rose quartz, and moonstone.

OSTARA INCENSE

Incense can be made using jasmine, frankincense, myrrh, cinnamon, nutmeg, orange peel, and rose petals. To any of these base ingredients you can add various gums or resins, such as gum Arabic or myrrh resin. Put your mixture into a small jar and label accordingly. This mixture can be sprinkled over charcoal disks.

OSTARA PURPOSE

A good spell for Ostara: cast your circle in the normal way (see page 41). While you are in your circle, write something that you are hoping to achieve on a piece of paper, then half-fill a large flowerpot with compost and lay the paper on top of it. Next, cover the paper with more compost until the pot is almost full. Finally, plant some sunflower seeds in the surface. Keep this pot in your circle even after your work has been done, and gradually your seeds should begin to sprout. As your seeds sprout and grow your plan should grow and develop. As with all rituals or ceremonies in the following pages, please feel free to amend them to suit your own needs, preferences, or purposes.

OSTARA RITUAL

Please refer to the instructions on page 41 (Samhain Ritual) to set up your circle. Then say these words or create your own:

The circle is about to be cast.
Let none be here but of their own free will.

Pick up your matches and move to the east and light the east candle saying:

Here do I bring into the east light and air to illuminate this circle and bring it the breath of life.

The south candle is lit saying:

Here do I bring into the south light and fire to illuminate this circle and bring it warmth.

The west candle is lit saying:

Here do I bring into the west light and water to illuminate this circle and wash it clean.

The north candle is lit saying:

Here do I bring into the north light and earth to illuminate this circle and build it in strength.

Return to your altar and say:

This circle line I now prepare,
Let no one enter should they dare.
This sacred space I dedicate,

Filled with love and never hate.
So mote it be.

Pick up your athame or wand or use the index finger of your dominant hand and draw the circle in the air, ſtarting at the eaſt, reaching the south, the weſt, then the north, and back to the eaſt. Next touch the salt on your altar with your athame, wand, or index finger and say:

As salt is life, let it purify me so that I may use it to cleanse my body and spirit in honor of the God and Goddess.

Put three pinches of salt in the water dish then raise your hand high, pointing your athame, wand, or index finger upwards, feeling the energy flowing into your arm. Put your athame, wand, or index finger into the water and ſtir three times, saying:

Salt is life, here is life, blessed be without strife, salt is life, here is life, blessed be without strife, salt is life, here is life, sacred be without strife.

Sprinkle the salted water around the circle edge ſtarting at the eaſt, moving to the south, the weſt, then the north, and back to the eaſt. Return to your altar and put down the consecrated water. Light any altar candles and your incense then pick up the athame, wand, or use your index finger to call the elemental guardians by drawing pentacles in the air, saying:

With air, fire, water, and earth I purify and charge you, east, hail guardians of the watchtower of the east, I invoke you [insert the name of the God or Goddess of your choice], come by the air that is your breath, may you stand in strength ever watching over this circle.

With fire, water, earth, and air I purify and charge you, south, hail guardians of the watchtower of the south, I invoke you [insert the name of the God or Goddess of your choice], come by the fire that is your spirit, may you stand in strength ever watching over this circle.

With water, earth, air, and fire I purify and charge you, west, hail guardians of the watchtower of the west, I invoke you [insert the name of the God or Goddess of your choice], come by the waters of your earthy womb that give us life, may you stand in strength ever watching over this circle.

With earth, air, fire, and water, I purify and charge you, north, hail guardians of the watchtower of the north, I invoke you [insert the name of the God or Goddess of your choice], come by the earth that is your body, may you stand in strength ever watching over this circle.

Take a drink from the chalice and focus your mind on the God and the Goddess. Then, standing in the Goddess position with your arms held high, invoke the Goddess energy into yourself and say:

> *Lady you have been known by many. I worship and adore you and invite you to join me in body and spirit. Be with me and guide me in the true ways.*

Pick up your athame, wand, or use your index finger and draw a pentacle in the air above you and below you and say:

> *You are here and I thank you for the gifts that you have given. I know that you only help those who help themselves. I say:*

> *I plant my seed that it may grow,*
> *My hopes within it, too, I sow.*
> *Dear Goddess see what I pursue,*
> *And help me see my dreams come true.*
> *If I deserve it through work and toil—*
> *Here symbolized by fertile soil—*
> *The day will come, through my volition,*
> *When I will see my work's fruition.*
> *An it harm none, do what thou will.*
> *What we send forth will return thrice over, so we send it forth with light and love.*
> *So mote it be.*

Visualize your prayers and wishes rising to the moon Goddess. Pick up the chalice or cup in your left hand and the athame or wand in your right hand and hold them at eye level, then place the point of the athame or wand or your index finger into the wine and say:

> *May male and female be joined and let all be fruitful throughout the land. The food I eat is the blessing of the Gods and I remember those who have none. I am grateful for all I have been given and am open and ready to receive that which is still to come.*
> *So mote it be.*
> *We have met in love and friendship, let us part the same way, spreading the love from this circle outward to all, sharing it with those we meet. Lord and Lady my thanks to you for sharing this time with me, guarding and guiding me.*
> *Merry we meet, merry we part, merry we meet again.*
> *The circle will now be closed.*

Finish with:

> *Take for your use, eastern watchtower, any powers of air that have not been used.*
> *Take for your use, southern watchtower, any powers of fire that have not been used.*
> *Take for your use, western watchtower, any powers of water that have not been used.*
> *Take for your use, northern watchtower, any powers of earth that have not been used.*
> *The circle is now closed but the work continues.*
> *Let it harm none, so mote it be.*

OSTARA FOODS

Foods associated with Ostara are eggs, honey, fruits, fish, cakes, cookies, fruit breads, cheeses, ham, sunflower seeds, sesame seeds, pine nuts, salad leaves, green vegetables, and some of the previous season's jams and preserves.

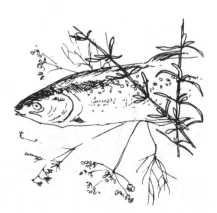

OSTARA RECIPES

FRENCH ONION SOUP

Serves 6 to 8

> Generous ⅓ cup (90 ml) extra-virgin olive oil
> 4½ lb (2 kg) onions, peeled and sliced
> 1 garlic bulb, peeled and sliced
> 1 teaspoon sugar
> 9½ cups (2.25 liters) stock (chicken, beef, or vegetable)
> 6–8 slices of crusty bread, toasted
>   (the amount depends on the amount of people you are serving)
> 4–6 oz (125–180 g) freshly grated cheese (your preference)

Warm the oil into a large soup pot over low heat then add the onions, garlic, and sugar and cook very slowly. (The sugar helps the onions to brown and prevents them from burning.) Keep stirring the onions frequently until they have all browned and reduced in size, 10–15 minutes. Cover the onions with the stock and simmer for 1 hour.

When you are near the end of this time, preheat the broiler. Put the toasted bread on a baking sheet, top with the grated cheese, and place under the broiler for 1–2 minutes until melted and browned. Ladle the soup into bowls, place a slice of cheesy toast on top of each, and serve.

EASTER SOUP

Serves 6 to 8

This is a very old recipe, an Italian broth known as *Brodetto Pasquale* (Easter broth), which is basically meat stock thickened with egg yolks. It marks the start of a traditional Roman Easter dinner. It is time consuming to make, but you are cooking your main course at the same time as you are making your soup. I like that! Serve the broth as a first course, and the stewed meat as your main course alongside potatoes and green vegetables or a salad.

> 1 lb (450 g) beef
> 1 lb (450 g) lamb
> 1 *bouquet garni* (A Magickal Bag, page 23)
> 1 onion, chopped
> 2 carrots, coarsely chopped
> 2 celery stalks, coarsely chopped
> 6 egg yolks
> Juice of ½ lemon
> 1 heaped teaspoon fresh marjoram, chopped
> 6–8 thin slices of Ciabatta Bread (page 213), toasted
>   (the amount depends on the amount of people you are serving)
> Salt and freshly ground black pepper
> Freshly grated Parmesan cheese, to serve

Place the meat in a large stockpot, add the *bouquet garni*, onion, carrots, and celery, generously cover with water. Bring to a boil, then reduce the heat to low and simmer gently for 3 hours.

Strain the stock, reserving the meat—you can shred this and serve it as a main dish. Skim off the fat from the surface of the stock and return it to the stockpot.

In a large bowl, beat the egg yolks with the lemon juice. Pour a ladleful of the stock over the beaten eggs, whisk well, then pour into stockpot and set over low heat. Gently simmer for 10–15 minutes until the soup thickens. Once thickened, add the marjoram and season to taste.

Line your soup bowls with the toasted ciabatta, ladle over the soup, and top with freshly grated Parmesan cheese.

NAAN BREAD

Serves 6 to 8

⅔ cup (150 ml) milk

¼ teaspoon saffron threads

1 teaspoon active-dry yeast

1 tablespoon sugar

2 cups (250 g) strong bread flour

A pinch of salt

2 tablespoons yogurt

2 tablespoons (30 g) melted butter or ghee,
    plus extra for greasing

Place 1 tablespoon of the milk in a small bowl with the saffron. Put the rest of the milk into a small saucepan. Bring to a boil, then turn off the heat and let it cool until it is just warm. Add the yeast and sugar to the warm milk and set aside for about 15 minutes, or until it froths a bit.

Meanwhile, mix the flour and, make a well in center, and add the yogurt, yeast solution, and saffron milk. Combine to make a light dough. (Flours can differ in their absorbency, so you might need to add a little water if it is too stiff.) No need to knead too much, since you are leaving it to rise overnight and the yeast will do all the work developing the gluten for you. Cover the dough with a warm wet cloth and leave in a warm place overnight.

When you are ready to cook, preheat the oven to its highest setting (450°F/230°C) or turn on your broiler. Grease a baking sheet with butter or ghee (or preheat a pizza stone if you have one). Split the dough into 6–8 balls then pat each ball into a tear shape (do this by hand rather than using a rolling pin). Place the naans on the baking sheet and stretch them gently, keeping the center slightly thinner than the edges. Bake or broil for 5 minutes, or until they have risen and are golden brown. Serve immediately with the melted butter or ghee, or reheat later. They freeze well too (but do so without the butter or ghee).

VARIATIONS: To make garlic naan, smear the naan with garlic butter or drizzle with garlic oil before baking. You can also top naan with cumin, fennel, poppy, nigella, or sesame seeds: press them into the dough when you are stretching them out. For a sweet version: halfway through their cooking time, remove the naans from the oven, let them cool a little, then split them open and sprinkle some brown sugar and dried shredded coconut inside. Close and reheat.

ROTI

Serves 6 to 8

½ cup (60 g) wholewheat flour
A pinch of salt
¼ cup (60 ml) water
¼ tsp olive oil
4 teaspoons melted butter or ghee (clarified butter)

Put the flour and salt into a bowl, add the water, and mix well with your fingers. Once the mixture has come together, rub your hands with the oil (this will stop the dough from sticking to you) and mix again. Break the dough into 4 even pieces and roll each piece out to a thin circle about 6 inches (15 cm) in diameter.

Heat a frying pan over very high heat, carefully place one roti in the pan, and cook for 1–2 minutes until brown spots appear on the underside and little air bubbles appear on the top. Turn the roti over and cook for another 2–3 minutes, using a spatula to press all around the edges. When it begins to puff up, it is ready.

Once the rotis are cooked, brush the tops with the melted butter and serve.

LAMB BHUNA

2 lb (900 g) boneless lamb shoulder, diced

6 tablespoons olive oil

3 large onions, finely chopped

1 teaspoon garlic paste

2 teaspoons ginger paste

3 fresh green chilies, chopped

1 teaspoon ground turmeric

2 tablespoons ground cumin

2 tablespoons ground coriander

1 teaspoon ground cayenne

3 medium tomatoes, skinned and chopped

Generous 1 cup (250 ml) warm water

1 teaspoon Garam Masala (page 45)

A good pinch of salt

Fresh cilantro, chopped, to garnish

Thoroughly rinse the lamb and set aside. Warm the oil in a large soup pot over medium-high heat. Add the onions and fry until just browned then add the garlic, ginger, and chilies and fry for a further 1–2 minutes.

Lower the heat to medium and stir in the turmeric, cumin, coriander, and cayenne. Slowly add the tomatoes and simmer the mixture for 2–3 minutes. Add the meat, stir, and simmer for 5 minutes, then add the water and bring to a boil.

Season with the salt then reduce the heat to low, cover, and simmer for 30–40 minutes, until slightly thickened and the meat is cooked. Add the garam masala and sprinkle with cilantro before serving. Serve with rice, Naan Bread (page 132), or Roti (page 133).

PEPPERED LAMB CHOPS

Serves 4

2–3 tablespoons coarsely crushed black peppercorns

6–8 small loin lamb chops

1 tablespoon extra-virgin olive oil

½ teaspoon salt

½ cup (125 ml) beef stock

¼ cup (60 ml) lemon juice

2 tablespoons (30 g) butter

1 tablespoon fresh rosemary leaves, chopped

Place the pepper on a large plate and press each chop firmly into the pepper on both sides.

Preheat the oven to 200°F (100°C). Heat the olive oil in a heavy frying pan (I use my cast-iron skillet) over medium-high heat, then sear the peppered lamb chops on both sides. Sprinkle the chops with the salt then reduce the heat to medium (do not deglaze the pan). Add the beef stock and lemon juice and continue to cook until the chops reach your desired temperature (2–3 minutes for medium-rare, 4–5 minutes for medium). Transfer the lamb chops to a heatproof serving platter and keep them warm in the oven.

Continue to cook the pan juices over medium heat, scraping any pieces of meat off the bottom of the pot and stirring them into the sauce. Let the liquid boil until it is reduced to a shiny glaze, about 10 minutes. Remove from the heat and whisk in the butter and fresh rosemary.

Remove the lamb chops from the oven and pour any lamb juices from the platter into the sauce. Spoon the sauce over the chops and serve.

HONEY-GLAZED HAM

Serves 4 to 6

2–3 lb (1–1.5 kg) boneless ham (cured or uncured)
2 tablespoons olive oil
2 tablespoons honey

Preheat the oven to 350°F (180°C). Rinse the ham under cold water, pat dry, then place it in a roasting pan and drizzle with the olive oil. Roast for 1 hour, then test if it is ready by piercing it with a sharp, pointed knife. If the meat is ready, the knife will slide in fairly easily and the tip of the knife will be hot against the back of your hand. If you have a meat thermometer, the center of the meat should be 160°F (70°C).

Increase the oven temperature to 475°F (250°C). Drizzle the honey over the top of the ham and put it back into the oven for a further 10 minutes.

Remove the ham from the oven and let it rest for about 10 minutes before slicing. If the ham is not being eaten immediately, let it cool completely before storing it in the refrigerator. Hot or cold, this is lovely with Cauliflower with Cheese (page 117) or vegetables in White Sauce flavored with parsley (page 31).

ORANGE-BAKED HAM

Serves 6 to 8

2–3 lb (1–1.5 kg) ham
2 tablespoons olive oil
3 large oranges, 1 thinly sliced, and 2 sliced into ½-inch
    (1½ cm) thick slices
6⅓ cups (1.5 liters) fresh orange juice

Preheat the oven to 350°F (180°C). Rinse the ham under cold water, pat dry, then place it in a roasting pan and drizzle with the olive oil. Cover with the thin orange slices and pour in the orange juice. Cover the ham with foil and roast in the oven for 1 hour.

Test if it is ready by piercing it with a sharp, pointed knife. If the meat is ready, the knife will slide in fairly easily and the tip of the knife will be hot against the back of your hand. If you have a meat thermometer, the center of the meat should be 160°F (70°C). When the ham is cooked, set it aside until it has rested and is cool enough to handle, about 30 minutes.

Turn up the oven temperature to 475°F (250°C). Slice the ham into ½-inch thick slices to match the thickness of the remaining orange slices. Now put the ham back together in the roasting pan in the following fashion: a slice of ham, a slice of orange, a slice of ham, a slice of orange, until you have used up all of the ham and oranges.

Baste the ham with the cooking juices and put it back in the oven for 10–15 minutes to heat through before serving.

HADDOCK IN BEER BATTER

Serves 4

Oil, for deep frying
4 medium haddock fillets (approx. 2 lb/900 g in total)
1 cup (125 g) all-purpose flour
A pinch of salt
A pinch of black pepper
1 cup (240 ml) beer
2 large eggs, 1 beaten

Rinse the fish and pat dry with paper towels.

In a bowl large enough to fit you fillets, combine a scant 1 cup (100 g) of the flour with the salt and pepper in a bowl large enough to fit your fillets. Make a well in the bowl of seasoned flour, add the second egg, and begin to mix it with a fork. Now add the beer, a little at a time, whisking with each addition. The batter should have a pouring consistency—not too thick, not too thin.

Fill your deep-fryer or a deep sauté pan with oil and set it over medium heat.

Put the remaining 3 tablespoons flour on a large plate, and place the beaten egg in a seperate large bowl. Take a fish fillet and first dip it in the beaten egg, then the flour, ensuring that both sides are well covered. Lastly, dip the fillet into the batter and make sure that it is well coated. Repeat with the remaining fillets.

Carefully place the fish fillet in the hot oil and cook for about 5 minutes (turning halfway through), until golden brown on each side. (Cook the fillets one at a time.) Remove from the oil and drain on paper towels before serving.

SMOKED HADDOCK FISH CAKES

Serves 2

2 medium to large pieces of smoked haddock (approx. 1 lb/450 g)

Milk, for poaching

A pat of butter

1 medium potato (approx. 6 oz/175 g), boiled and mashed

2–3 slices of fresh bread, toasted if you like

½ cup (60 g) all-purpose flour

1 egg, beaten

½ cup (125 ml) sunflower or vegetable oil,
    or more if needed, for frying

Salt and freshly ground black pepper

Herbs or spices appropriate to any ritual you are working on (optional)

In a large saucepan, cover the smoked haddock with milk, add the butter, and cook over high heat for 3–4 minutes, until the fish flakes easily. Set aside to cool completely and drain.

Flake the fish and mix it with the potatoes using your hands. Shape into small palm-sized cakes about 1 inch (2.5 cm) thick. Set aside while you prepare the breadcrumbs.

Make the bread (either toasted or untoasted; your preference) into breadcrumbs using a blender, food processor, or fine grater. Place in a bowl.

Place the flour in another bowl, along with salt and pepper to taste and any herbs or spices, if using. Place the egg into another bowl.

Dip a fish cake first into the flour, then into the egg, and finally into the breadcrumbs. When all the fish cakes have been coated, set a frying pan over medium-high heat and warm enough oil to fry the cakes. When the oil is hot, fry for 2–3 minutes on each side until they are golden brown, working in batches if you have to. Transfer to a plate lined with paper towels and serve hot.

OMELET

Serves 2 to 3

3 eggs
1 teaspoon water
A good pinch of salt and freshly ground black pepper
(or adjust to suit your taste)
1 tablespoon butter or olive oil

Set a nonstick frying pan over medium-high heat. Break the eggs into a bowl and whisk thoroughly then add the water and salt and pepper and whisk again.

When the pan is very hot, add the butter or oil. Pour the eggs into the pan and let them sit for a few seconds to set on the bottom. Using a spatula, push the sides into the middle of the pan and allow the loose egg to run to the outside. Let it sit for a few seconds to set again and then repeat this process if necessary.

When the omelet is cooked through, fold one half over the other, slide onto a plate, and serve immediately. You could also skip folding the omelet and place the pan under the broiler for 1–2 minutes until browned and risen, then serve immediately.

VARIATIONS:

1. Tomato omelet: Dice 2 tomatoes and add to the egg mixture as soon as you put it in the pan. Cook as above.

2. Cheese and onion omelet: Grate cheese (of your choice) and peel and finely dice 1 onion and add to the egg mixture as soon as you put it in the pan. Cook as above.

3. Bacon omelet: First cut a few slices of bacon into small pieces and fry until they are crispy. Add to the egg mixture in the pan. Cook as above.

HERB EGGS

Serves 4 to 6

6 eggs, hardboiled and shelled
2 tablespoons Mayonnaise (page 33)
1 garlic clove, crushed
A handful of your favorite herbs
Salt and freshly ground black pepper
Paprika or other ground spices, to garnish

Carefully slice the eggs in half lengthwise so that the two halves separate. Carefully remove the yolks and place them in a bowl. Place the whites on a tray with the hole facing up.

Mash the egg yolks, adding the mayonnaise a little at a time until you reach a consistency that you like. Season with the garlic, herbs, and salt and pepper to taste. Then fill the whites with the yolk mixture (you could use a piping bag if you have one). Garnish with paprika or other spices that suit your ritual work.

CURRIED EGGS

Serves 4 to 6

6 eggs, hardboiled and shelled
2 tablespoons Mayonnaise (page 33)
1 garlic clove, crushed
2 heaped teaspoons strong curry powder
Salt and freshly ground black pepper
Paprika or other ground spices, to garnish

Carefully slice the eggs in half lengthwise so that the two halves separate. Carefully remove the yolks and place them in a bowl. Place the whites on a tray with the hole facing up.

Mash the egg yolks, adding the mayonnaise a little at a time until you reach a consistency that you like. Season with the garlic, curry powder, and salt and pepper to taste then fill the whites with the yolk mixture and garnish to suit your ritual work.

SPICY RAISIN PASTA SALAD

Serves 4 to 6

8 oz (250 g) macaroni
⅔–¾ (90–115 g) cups raisins (or any combination of dried fruits)
1 tablespoon curry powder
Salt and freshly ground black pepper
Approx. ½ cup (115 g) Mayonnaise (page 33)
Salt

Cook the macaroni in a large saucepan of boiling salted water for 8–10 minutes, or until cooked to your liking. Drain and set aside to cool.

When the macaroni is cool, add the raisins (or dried fruit), curry powder, and salt and pepper to taste then mix well. Add the mayonnaise a tablespoon at a time until the pasta is lightly coated. Stir again before serving.

SEED, PETALS, AND PASTA SALAD

Serves 4 to 6

12 oz (375 g) pasta of your choice
1 tablespoon olive oil
1 garlic clove, crushed
2 tablespoons sunflower petals
1 tablespoon sunflower seeds
1 tablespoon chives, chopped
Nasturtium or pansy petals, to garnish (optional)
Salt

Bring a large pot of salted water to a boil, add the pasta, and cook until "al dente" (about 8–10 minutes or follow the package instructions). Drain and set aside.

Heat the oil in a large frying pan over medium-high heat, add the garlic, and toss in the cooked pasta. Stir well, remove from the heat, and pour into a serving bowl. Add the sunflower petals, sunflower seeds, and chives and garnish with fresh nasturtium or pansy petals, if using. Serve warm or cold.

POTATO SALAD WITH CHIVES OR MINT *Serves 4 to 6*

> 3 lb (1.5 kg) potatoes (any kind), peeled, boiled, and cubed
>
> 2 tablespoons Mayonnaise (page 33), or more if needed
>
> Fresh chives or mint (or any herb of your preference), chopped, to taste
>
> Salt and freshly ground black pepper, to taste

Combine all your ingredients together and stir well. Add additional mayonnaise, if needed, to reach your desired consistency. Chill before serving.

HERBY POTATOES

Serves 4 to 6

> 3 lb (1.5 kg) baby potatoes, washed
>
> 4 tablespoons (60 g) butter
>
> Chopped herbs of your preference, to taste
>> (I recommend rosemary, parsley, or mint)

Place the potatoes in a large pot, cover with water, and bring to a boil. Reduce the heat to low and simmer for 20 minutes, or until they can be easily pierced with a knife.

Drain the water and put the potatoes into a serving bowl with the butter. Once the better has melted, add the herbs, give everything a stir, and serve immediately.

AVOCADO SALAD

Serves 2

Your avocado should feel like an orange would when you press it. The avocado stone can be saved and planted as a house plant. I have one that is now four feet tall! Pop it into a small pot of compost two thirds under the soil and water it occasionally.

> 1 avocado
> 4–6 large lettuce leaves of your preference, chopped
> ½ cup (70 g) pine nuts
> 1 tablespoon chopped herbs (such as parsley, mint, or chamomile)
> Olive oil
> Lemon juice
> Salt and freshly ground black pepper

Peel and cut the avocado into bite-size pieces. To do this, take a sharp knife and cut along the length all the way around, right through to the stone. Hold the avocado between the palms of your hands and twist in opposite directions—it will split. Pop out the stone by carefully chopping into it deeply with a sharp knife and twisting. If ripe, the flesh should scoop out easily (or you can peel away the skin). Or hold one side of the avocado in the palm of your hand, flesh side up, and slice through the flesh from top to bottom but not through the skin. Repeat this cut from side to side then turn it inside out. You will find that the fruit just peels away from the skin.

Put the chopped leaves into a salad bowl. Toss in the pine nuts and herbs and set aside. Add the avocado pieces. Drizzle with olive oil and lemon juice, season to taste, and thoroughly mix all the ingredients together, adding more oil or lemon juice if needed. Serve immediately.

CABBAGE WITH LEMON AND GARLIC *Serves 4 to 6*

2 tablespoons olive oil

1 garlic bulb, split into cloves and peeled

1 medium cabbage, core removed, shredded

1 teaspoon salt

1 whole lemon, cut in half

Set a large skillet or sauté pan (use one that has a lid) over medium heat and add the oil. Gently fry the garlic cloves for 1–2 minutes then add the cabbage and salt and place the lid on the pan. After 10 minutes, remove the lid and stir, then replace the lid and continue to cook for 30 minutes, removing the lid every 10 minutes to stir. Do not worry if the cabbage becomes brown—this adds to the flavor.

Once the cabbage has cooked, squeeze the lemon juice from one half all over the cabbage, stir, and serve immediately, with the other lemon half on the side in case someone wants more lemon juice.

LEMON MERINGUE PIE

Serves 4 to 6

> 1 portion Shortcrust Pastry (page 28)
> 1¼ cups (300 ml) cold water
> 3 tablespoons cornstarch
> Scant 1¼ cups (220 g) organic sugar, plus extra for sprinkling
> Zest and juice of 2 large unwaxed lemons
> 3 large eggs (separated)
> 2 tablespoons (30 g) butter
> Scant 1 cup (180 g) superfine sugar
> Whipped cream, to serve (optional)

Rest your shortcrust pastry in the refrigerator for 1 hour. Preheat the oven to 400°F (200°C). Roll out the pastry to a thickness of about ¼ inch (0.5 cm), making sure it is big enough to cover the bottom and sides of a 9-inch (23 cm) pie dish (trim off any excess). Use the pastry to line the dish, cover with parchment paper, weigh it down with pie weights (or just use dried beans or peas), and blind bake for 10 minutes. Remove from the oven and reduce the temperature to 350°F (180°C).

Place a few tablespoons of the cold water into a jug, add the cornstarch and ⅓ cup (60 g) of the sugar, and blend. Pour the rest of the water and the lemon juice and zest into a saucepan, bring to a boil, and then pour it into the jug with the cornstarch, stirring all the time.

Return the mixture to the saucepan and bring it back to a boil, stirring continuously. Turn the heat to low and simmer the mixture very gently for 1 minute, stirring continuously to prevent it from sticking. Remove the pan from the heat and beat in the egg yolks, then the butter. Pour the lemon mixture into the pastry shell and spread it out evenly.

Using an electric mixer or whisk, and a spotlessly clean glass bowl, beat the egg whites until they form stiff peaks, then whisk in a quarter of the superfine sugar at a time until all has been added. Spread the meringue over the lemon mixture to the very edge of the pastry rim, then sprinkle with a little extra sugar.

Bake in the oven on the center rack for 45 minutes, by which time the meringue will have turned pale beige and be crisp on the outside. Serve hot or cold with whipped cream.

LAVENDER RICE PUDDING

Serves 4 to 6

2½ cups (600 ml) whole milk

1 large sprig of lavender, bruised

4 oz (125 g) short-grain white rice

⅓ cup (60 g) sugar

2 pats of butter

12 oz (350 g) can evaporated milk

2 tablespoons (30 g) butter

Preheat the oven to 350°F (180°C). Put the milk in a small saucepan over low heat, add the lavender, and heat gently to infuse the milk with the lavender for 4 minutes, then remove (and reserve) the sprig.

Rinse the rice in a sieve under cold running water then place it in a deep 6-inch (15 cm) round baking dish (or any baking dish with a 4-cup/1-liter capacity; if larger, it will impact the bake time). Add the sugar and infused milk, mix everything together, add a pat of butter, then stir again. Lay the lavender sprig on the top of the mixture. Bake until the milk starts simmering, about 10 minutes, then reduce the heat to 275°F (140°C) and cook the pudding slowly for 2 hours, until soft and thickened. After 1 hour, add the evaporated milk and another pat of butter then continue to bake for the remaining 1 hour. Serve warm or cold.

LAVENDER CUSTARD

Serves 2

Generous 1 cup (250 ml) milk, plus 1 teaspoon
2 sprigs of lavender
1 tablespoon cornstarch
1 egg, beaten
2 teaspoons sugar

Put the cup of milk in a small saucepan over low heat, add the lavender, and heat gently to infuse the milk with the lavender for 4 minutes, then remove the sprigs.

In a heatsafe mixing bowl, blend the cornstarch with the teaspoon of cold milk. Pour the heated milk over the cornstarch then return the mixture to the saucepan over medium heat. Stir until it boils, then boil gently for 1 minute.

Remove from the heat, cool slightly, and pour over the beaten egg. Return the mixture to the heat and stir over low heat until the mixture thickens (do not boil it), about 5 minutes.

Add the sugar and stir until dissolved, then remove from the heat to cool slightly before serving. If serving the custard cold, cover the surface with plastic wrap while cooling to avoid a skin forming.

LAVENDER CRÈME BRÛLÉE

Serves 6

4 egg yolks
6 tablespoons sugar
Generous 1 cup (250 ml) whipping cream
4 small top sprigs of fresh lavender
Butter, for greasing

Preheat the oven to 300°F (150°C) and grease six small ramekins (about 5 oz/150 ml capacity). Using an electric hand mixer or a stand mixer, beat the egg yolks with 4 tablespoons of the sugar. Add the cream and mix thoroughly then divide this mixture among the ramekins.

Place the ramekins in a deep pan. Fill the pan with enough warm water so that it comes halfway up the ramekins. Bake for 40–45 minutes, until the mixtures are set around the edges but wobbly in the middle.

Remove the pan from the oven and set aside until the ramekins are cool to the touch. Heat your broiler. Sprinkle the remaining 2 tablespoons of sugar over the tops of each ramekin and place under the broiler for 1–2 minutes, until the sugar bubbles. Refrigerate until cold then serve.

SUNFLOWER SEED BREAD

Makes 2 small loaves

You can substitute sesame seeds or pine nuts for sunflower seeds in this bread.

7½ cups (900 g) white bread flour, plus extra for dusting

4 tablespoons (60 g) butter, softened

2 tablespoons sunflower seeds

2 teaspoons sugar (optional, but the sugar will create a nice crust)

2 teaspoons salt

2 envelopes (14 g) instant yeast

1¼ cups (300 ml) cold water

1¼ cups (300 ml) boiling water

Vegetable oil, for greasing

Follow the method on page 30 to make 2 small loaves or rounds.

BELTANE

We jump the fire and celebrate love,
We jump the fire and celebrate life.
This fertile land will bring us fruits,
This cleansing fire ends winter's Strife.

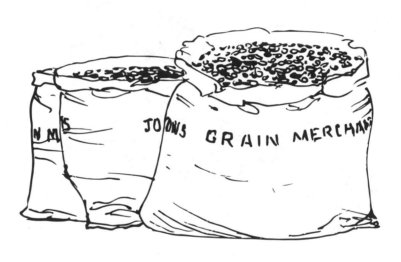

CHAPTER SIX

BELTANE

APRIL 30TH, AND MAY DAY: 1ST SUNDAY IN MAY

When I was growing up I knew nothing about Beltane, but I did know about the "first Sunday in May." My family were Christians, and on May Day I got something new to wear. I have no idea if that's what happened in other households but I always got a new dress for May Day.

For pagans, Beltane is a fire festival and a time to celebrate the joy of fertility. Fires are lit in cauldrons and pagans jump the "Bel" fire. The weather improves, the land is becoming fertile and full of life, and generally everyone is happier. As we celebrate the love and union of the Goddess and the God, romance is in the air; people often plan weddings to celebrate their love for each other at this time. As pagans, we have a "handfasting" (wedding), and for those of us already joined, May Day is a good time to have our baby blessed in a naming ceremony (a pagan baptism).

The Maypole is the traditional symbol of Beltane. Some English, German, and Austrian communities still dance around the Maypole, and have other celebrations on May 1st.

BELTANE CRYSTALS

Crystals associated with Beltane are rose quartz, blue lace agate, bloodstones, aventurine, moonstone, and carnelian.

BELTANE COLORS

Colors associated with Beltane are pink, red, white, and green.

BELTANE INCENSE

Incense can be made using dried rose, vanilla, primrose, hawthorn, birch, rosemary, frankincense, ivy, and marigolds. To any of these base ingredients you can add various gums or resins, such as gum Arabic or myrrh resin. Put your mixture into a small jar and label accordingly. This mixture can be sprinkled over charcoal disks.

BELTANE PURPOSE

This time of year is all about love, romance, and fertility and is a perfect time for handfasting ceremonies (weddings) and naming ceremonies. As with all rituals or ceremonies in the following pages, please feel free to amend them to suit your own needs, preferences, or purposes.

BELTANE NAMING CEREMONY RITUAL

I prepared this circle for one of my readers and the role of high priestess was performed by the grandmother. If you have another family member who would like to carry out the naming ceremony for your child, please feel free to adapt the following to suit your needs. If there are two grandparents they can of course both be involved in the ceremony.

You should prepare your circle as follows, as well as blessing cards for each of your guests so they can write down their blessings for your baby. Gifts should be non-tangible, such as health, beauty, skills, and such. The circle should be cast in your usual fashion (see Samhain Ritual, page 41; use a semicircle if your space is small), and an inner circle should be cast for the high priestess (in this case, the grandmother), as well as the parents, godparents, and baby. The guests should remain in the outer circle. A doorway should be left open in the inner circle with an archway if possible. The parents and godparents should be standing at the edges of the inner circle with females to the left and males to the right.

The high priestess calls upon the lord and lady to witness the blessing and when she is ready she invites the mother and father (without the baby) into the circle. She places her hands on the top of each of their heads and blesses the mother and father in her own words. When this done the mother stands to her left and the father stands to her right. The grandmother calls:

Who stands for this child?

The godparent or godparents answer:

I/we do.

The high priestess welcomes them with the baby into the circle. The godfather holds the baby while the grandmother places her hand on the godmother's head and blesses her. The godmother then holds the baby while the godfather receives a similar blessing.

The high priestess takes the baby from the godmother and holds it high and presents the child to the lord and lady and blesses the child with gifts of health and happiness (or whatever she wishes) finishing with:

I name this child [insert the baby's name], may she/he live a long and healthy life filled with joy.

With this done, she carries the baby to the first guest and places the baby in the guest's arms. They hold the baby, and looking into the baby's eyes, bless the baby saying:

I bless [the baby's name] with the gift of [insert gift].

They then pass the baby to the next guest who does the same. The baby is passed round all the guests and finally given back to the high priestess who passes the baby to the mother. The high priestess thanks the lord and lady for witnessing the blessing and closes the circle.

BELTANE HANDFASTING CEREMONY

Before the guests arrive, the circle should be cast (see Samhain Ritual, page 41), leaving a doorway open to allow the guests to enter.

The best man/priest should stand to the right of the opening and the best maid/priestess should stand to the left of the opening. As the guests line up to enter, the best man/priest should take the first female guest's hand and say:

In what manner do you enter this circle?

She should reply:

In perfect truth and perfect love.

The best man/priest should "pull" her into the circle and she should walk all the way around the circle in a clockwise direction until she reaches the best man/priest. The best maid/priestess should take the first male guest's hand and say:

In what manner do you enter this circle?

He should reply:

In perfect truth and perfect love.

The best maid/priestess should "pull" him into the circle and he should walk all the way around the circle in a clockwise direction until he reaches the first female guest.

This process should be repeated until all the guests are assembled, at which point the best man/priest and the best maid/priestess should leave the circle to fetch the bride and groom. The best maid/priestess brings the groom into the circle and walks around the circle clockwise then back to the altar and places him to the right of the altar. The best man/priest brings the bride into the circle and walks around the circle clockwise then back to the altar and places her to the left of the altar.

The high priestess raises her arms to the sky and says:
> *We gather in this scared place*
> *And stand together face to face.*
> *Our promises we make today*
> *Never broken come what may.*

The groom says:
> *Without you my days are dark and empty and my nights are long and cold.*

The bride says:
> *Without you I have no purpose, no future to unfold.*

The groom says:
> *Join me, make my life complete.*

The bride says:
> *With you my life's replete.*

The groom says:
> *I [insert groom's name] promise to love, cherish, and adore you from this day forth.*

The bride says:
> *I [insert bride's name] promise to love, cherish, and adore you from this day forth.*

The high priestess holds a censer of incense high in front of the bride and groom and asks:
> *In what manner do you make this promise?*

Facing the east, the bride and groom say:
> *By the air that we breathe we make this promise.*

The high priestess replaces the censer of incense and raises a candle high in front of the bride and groom and says:

In what manner do you make this promise?

Facing the south, the bride and groom say:

By the fire in our loins we make this promise.

The high priestess replaces the candle and sprinkles the bride and groom with consecrated water and asks:

In what manner do you make this promise?

Facing the west, the bride and groom say:

By the water that gives us life, we make this promise.

The high priestess replaces the consecrated water and holds a dish of soil in front of the bride and groom and asks:

In what manner do you make this promise?

Facing the north, the bride and groom say:

By the earth that holds our weight we make this promise.

The high priestess hands a chalice of wine to the bride and an athame or wand to the groom and they turn and face each other. The high priestess holds her hands up high and invokes the God and the Goddess while the best man/priest and best maid/priestess take the wedding rings and drop them into the wine. The high priestess says:

May the Lord and Lady and all here present witness this rite and may [insert bride's name] and [insert the groom's name] be joined together.

May the Lord and Lady bless this union so that it be fruitful and filled with love.

As the high priestess says these words the groom should place the athame or wand into the wine and remain in that position until the high priestess is ready. In this fashion may man and woman be joined.

The high priestess asks:

Where are the rings?

The groom uses the point of the athame or wand to remove the rings from the chalice. The best maid/priestess steps forward with the consecrated water and the high priestess rinses the bride's ring in the water and offers it to the groom who places it on the bride's finger. The high priestess rinses the groom's ring in the water and offers it to the bride who places it on the groom's finger. The best man/priest then steps forward with a white cord or ribbon and the high priestess wraps the cords in a figure eight round the bride and groom's wrists and ties them. She says:

> *As these rings represent the circle that binds your love so too do these cords represent the circle that binds your lives together.*
>
> *By the power and the blessings of the Lord and Lady you are now joined as husband and wife.*

The bride and groom kiss.

The best man/priest and best maid/priestess lay a broomstick on the ground and the bride and the groom jump the broomstick.

BELTANE FOODS

Foods associated with Beltane are all dairy foods particularly eggs, as well as grains and oats. Foods containing honey and fruits, and salad dishes containing edible petals, roses, calendula, nasturtiums, and pansies are all acceptable.

BELTANE RECIPES

CREAM OF LETTUCE SOUP

Serves 4 to 6

This is a really lovely recipe that comes in handy if you have grown or bought too much lettuce.

> 1 large head of lettuce, coarsely chopped
> 1 medium carrot, peeled and coarsely chopped
> 1 medium potato, peeled and coarsely chopped
> 4¼ cups (1 liter) ham stock (page 25)
> A pinch of salt and freshly ground black pepper
> (or adjust to suit your taste)
> ½ cup (125 ml) cream, to serve

Place the vegetables and stock in a stockpot over high heat, season to your liking, and bring to a boil. Turn the heat down to low, cover the pot, and simmer for at least 30 minutes until all the vegetables are very tender.

Once cooked, set the soup aside to cool then purée using a blender, food processor, or hand-held immersion blender until smooth. Taste and adjust the seasoning if needed then reheat in the stockpot over low heat. Just before serving, stir in the cream.

LEMON CHICKEN

Serves 8

This dish can be prepared in a variety of ways. You can fry the chicken in a batter, as below; or dip the chicken in melted butter then in seasoned flour before frying in butter, to produce a nicely golden, slightly crisp coating; or simply fry the chicken in butter without a flour or batter coating. All go well with the flavorful lemon sauce. This dish works well with rice and a side salad.

8 medium chicken breasts
Olive oil, for frying

Batter
2 eggs, beaten
A good pinch of salt
A good pinch of pepper
½ cup (90 g) cornstarch
¼ cup (60 ml) water

Lemon Sauce
1½ cups (375 ml) water
½ cup (125 ml) lemon juice
Scant ⅔ cup (125 g) light brown sugar
½ cup (90 g) cornstarch
3 tablespoons honey
¼ teaspoon ground ginger
Salt and freshly ground black pepper

Make the batter: In a bowl, combine the eggs, salt, pepper, and cornstarch. Gradually add the water, stirring continuously, until you have a uniform batter. Dip the chicken breasts into the batter, making sure they are well coated.

In a large frying pan set over high heat, fry the chicken breasts in a splash of olive oil until they are cooked, 2–3 minutes on each side (you might need to do this in batches). You can test the chicken by piercing the flesh with a skewer or a sharp, pointed knife—the juice that runs out should be clear and, if using a knife, the point should be very hot to the touch. If you have a meat thermometer, the internal temperature should be 165°F (75°C).

Meanwhile, prepare the lemon sauce. Combine all of the sauce ingredients in a small saucepan over medium heat, stirring continuously until the sauce boils. Reduce the heat to low and simmer for 5 minutes, or until slightly thickened. Taste and adjust the seasoning if needed.

To serve, the chicken breasts can be left whole or sliced into bite-sized pieces. The sauce is best served in a little dish on the side of each plate, but it can also be drizzled over the chicken.

Spanish Omelet

Serves 2 to 3

      Olive oil, for frying
      ¾ cup (85 g) leftover boiled potatoes, diced
      1 red or green bell pepper, diced
      1 onion, chopped
      4 eggs, beaten
      A pinch of salt and freshly ground black pepper
         (or adjust to suit your taste)
      Fresh herbs (your preference), to garnish
      Buttered toast, to serve (optional)

Warm a splash of olive oil in a frying pan over high heat and fry the potatoes until they are crisp on all sides. Add the pepper and onion and fry for 2 minutes, then add the eggs, salt, and pepper. Do not stir; wait for the eggs to set on the bottom, then stir to bring the set egg to the top and allow the uncooked egg to run to the bottom of the pan. Repeat this procedure until your eggs are totally cooked.

Serve at once garnished with additional seasoning (if needed), your favorite herbs, and buttered toast.

CREAMY GUACAMOLE

Serves 2 to 3

This is a rich, creamy version of guacamole that uses cream cheese. It should be made just before you wish to serve it, since mashed avocados have a tendency to turn brown (the addition of the lemon or lime juice helps to slow this process down). Serve with chips.

> 2 medium tomatoes
> Boiling water
> 2 ripe avocados
> 12 oz (350 g) cream cheese (1½ cups)
> Juice of ½ lemon or lime
> Salt and freshly ground black pepper

Skin the tomatoes: Make a small slit in the skin of each and then drop them into a bowl of boiling water. After a minute or two, the fruit will swell and the skin will shrink, exposing the flesh. Remove from the water and peel off the skin. (The skin can also be removed by piercing a fork into the tomato and carefully holding it over a gas flame.) Cut the tomatoes in half and discard the seeds. Finely dice them and set aside.

Remove the avocado flesh (see page 144 for my method) and mash it with a fork. You should decide at this point whether your guacamole is going to be coarse or smooth (I like coarse). When the avocado is mashed to your desired consistency, add the tomatos and cream cheese and mix well. Add the lemon juice and season with salt and pepper, then taste and adjust the ingredients to your liking.

BELTANE SALAD

Serves 3 to 4

1 lb (450 g) baby spinach

1–2 cups (55–85 g) young dandelion leaves or arugula

1 cucumber, diced

4 scallions, chopped

A few strawberries, sliced

Dressing

2 tablespoons white wine vinegar

2 tablespoons olive oil

1 teaspoon English mustard

1 garlic clove, chopped

1 tablespoon honey

Salt and freshly ground black pepper

Combine all the salad ingredients in a large bowl. Whisk together the dressing ingredients and season to taste. Dress the salad with just enough dressing to coat all the leaves and serve immediately.

CRYSTALIZED PETALS

1 egg white, beaten

Edible petals, rinsed and dried

Sugar, for sprinkling

In a small bowl, combine the egg white and a few drops of water and whisk together. Dip each flower petal in the egg mixture. Sprinkle with sugar and place on a wire cooling rack set over a baking tray. Set aside for a few hours until firm and set. Use as garnishes for sweet and savory dishes.

POT MARIGOLD CUSTARD

Serves 4

Pot marigold (calendula) petals have many uses (see pages 21 and 251). I harvest my petals during the flowering season. They have a long flowering season and are one of the easier flowers to grow—sow them in spring and they will blossom during beltane. You can also dry them and store them in an airtight jar for year-round use.

> 1 tablespoon cornstarch
>
> Generous 1¾ cups (450 ml) cold milk
>
> A handful of pot marigold (calendula) petals (fresh or dried)
>
> 1 egg, beaten
>
> 2 teaspoons sugar
>
> A few drops vanilla extract
>
> Heavy cream, for drizzling
>
> Fresh pot marigold petals or Crystalized Petals (page 163),
>   to garnish

Using an electic hand mixer or stand mixer, blend the cornstarch with 2 tablespoons of the milk. Gently heat the remaining milk and marigold petals in a saucepan over low heat (if you heat it too quickly the milk might burn). Mix a ladleful of the hot milk into the cornstarch mixture, then return the mixture to the pan. Bring to a boil then reduce the heat and simmer for 1 minute.

Remove the pan from the heat and cool the mixture slightly, before adding the well-beaten egg. Return the pan to the heat and stir the mixture over low heat until it thickens, but make sure it does not boil. This should only take 1–2 minutes.

Once the custard has thickened, add the sugar and vanilla and stir until dissolved.

To serve, put the custard into a serving bowl, drizze a little heavy cream into the center, and sprinkle with fresh or crystalized petals.

MERINGUES

Makes approx. 12

4 large organic eggs, separated
Scant ⅔ cup (125 g) sugar
1 cup (125 g) confectioners' sugar
Whipped cream, for serving

Preheat the oven to 212°F (100°C). Line two baking sheets with nonstick liners or parchment paper.

Put the egg whites into a large, spotlessly clean glass mixing bowl. Using an electric hand mixer or stand mixer, beat them on medium speed until the mixture resembles a fluffy cloud and stands up in stiff peaks when the blades are lifted out. Turn the speed up and start to add the sugar, a little at a time. (It is important to add the sugar slowly at this stage—it helps prevent the meringue from weeping later.) Continue beating for 3–4 seconds between each addition, but do not over-mix. When ready, the mixture should be thick and glossy and if you hold the bowl upside down, it should not move.

Sift one-third of the confectioners' sugar over the mixture, then gently fold it in with a big metal spoon or rubber spatula. Continue to sift and fold in the confectioners' sugar a third at a time, again being careful not to over-mix. The mixture should now look smooth and billowy.

Using a dessertspoon with a pointed end, scoop out a (2–3 tablespoon size) dollop of the mixture. Using another spoon, ease the meringue mixture onto the baking sheet to make an oval shape, or just drop it in rough rounds if you prefer. Repeat until the mixture is used up.

Bake for 1½–1¾ hours—the meringues should be a pale beige color and sound crisp when tapped on the bottom. Leave to cool completely on the baking sheet or a cooling rack.

Meringues will keep in an airtight container for up to 2 weeks or frozen for a month. Serve two meringues sandwiched together with whipped cream, if you like.

HANDFASTING CAKE

Serves 6 to 8

9 tablespoons (125 g) butter, plus extra for greasing

Scant 1 cup (180 g) sugar

2 tablespoons honey

1 tablespoon rose water or other flower water (please make sure
it is not alcohol-based; use a mild, water-based flower water),
plus extra for the topping

4 eggs

1⅔ cups (180 g) self-rising flour

½ teaspoon baking powder

1 cup (120 g) confectioners' sugar

2 tablespoons fresh rose petals

Preheat the oven to 350°F (180°C). In a large mixing bowl, cream the butter and sugar using an electric hand mixer or stand mixer until fluffy and light. Add the honey and rose water and mix well. Add the eggs, one at a time, beating well after each addition, then fold in the flour and baking powder.

Grease an 8-inch (20 cm) cake pan then pour in the batter and bake for 1 hour. Check if it is ready by inserting a skewer in the center of the cake; if it comes out clean, is it done. Let the cake cool completely before removing from the pan.

For the icing, mix the confectioners' sugar with just enough flower water to create a loose pouring consistency (1–2 tablespoons). Cover the top of the cake with the icing, then decorate with fresh rose petals while the icing is still wet. Leave to set before serving.

HONEY CAKE

Serves 4 to 6

1 cup (225 g) butter, plus extra for greasing
Scant ¾ cup (175 ml) clear honey, plus 1 tablespoon
½ cup (100 g) brown sugar
A pinch of saffron
3 large eggs, beaten
1⅓ cup (300 g) self-rising flour
Sugar, for sprinkling

Preheat the oven to 325°F (160°C). Grease and line an 8-inch (20 cm) round cake pan with parchment paper.

Melt the butter, honey, and brown sugar together in a saucepan over medium heat until runny, about 2 minutes, then bring to a boil and cook for 1 minute. Add the saffron and set aside to cool.

Add the eggs into the cooled honey mixture and mix well. Add the flour and mix thoroughly until smooth. Pour into the cake pan (it should be quite runny), sprinkle the top with sugar, and bake on the center rack in the oven for 50 minutes. Check if it is ready by inserting a skewer in the center of the cake; if it comes out clean, is it done.

When cooked, turn the cake out of the pan and, while still warm, brush the top with the tablespoon of honey. Leave to cool on a wire rack.

Serve with a glass of May Wine (page 168) or Nectar (page 121).

MAY WINE

Serves 4

4 green cardamom pods
6 oz (180 g) raspberries
1 bottle (750 ml) white wine (preferably German Riesling)
1 lemon, sliced, to serve
A few sprigs fresh mint, to serve
A few nasturtium flowers, to serve

Crush the cardamom pods lightly with a mortar and pestle and put them in a large jug. Add the raspberries and the wine and leave overnight to steep.

The next day, pour the contents of the jug into a jelly bag or a cheesecloth suspended over a bowl. Set aside for at least 1 hour. Decant the contents of the bowl into a serving jug.

Serve with ice, lemon slices, mint, and nasturtium flowers.

FLOWER PUNCH

Serves 4

2 cups (30 g) edible flower petals (see page 21)
1 bottle (750 ml) sweet white wine (German Riesling is good, but
    you can use your favorite)

Once you have gathered all your petals, soak them in the wine and refrigerate for 1 hour. Serve with some petals still floating in the wine.

Alternatively, if you need to make it ahead of time, you can refrigerate the petals and wine for up to 2 days, but before serving, strain the wine through a sieve and add some fresh petals.

ELDERFLOWER CORDIAL

Makes approx. 1 cup (240 ml)

Elderflowers are in season in May and June. If you miss out on the blossoms, look for the elderberries from August to September, from which you can make jellies and wine. This versatile mixture can be used as a healing syrup, refreshing drink, flavoring for cakes, or in spellwork.

> About 10 elderflower heads
> Juice of 1 lemon
> 1 tablespoon honey

Rinse the elderflower heads under cold running water then remove as much green stem as you can. Place them in a small saucepan and add just enough water to cover the elderflowers. Bring to a boil and then reduce the heat to low and simmer for 20 minutes.

Strain the liquid and discard the flowers then put the liquid back in the pan and add the lemon juice and honey. Bring to a boil then turn the heat to low and simmer for 5–10 minutes, until it thickens slightly. Turn off the heat and set aside to cool. Bottle and store in the refrigerator for up to 1 month.

This mixture has several uses:

1. Take an undiluted teaspoon 3 times a day if you have a cough, cold, or sore throat.

2. For a refreshing drink, add a tablespoon to a glass of water.

3. Add to cake mixes for flavor or to complement any ritual or spell that you may be working on.

CHERRY SAUCE

Serves 4

This sauce makes a nice accompaniment to roast turkey, chicken, goose, or duck. Alternatively, you can freeze fresh cherries in season and make this sauce at Yule.

> 3¼ cups (500 g) cherries, fresh or frozen
> 1½ cups (375 ml) cold water
> ½ cup (100 g) sugar
> ½ cup (125 ml) orange juice
> 1 tablespoon cornstarch

Wash some jam jars in hot soapy water then sterilize them (see page 57).

If using frozen cherries, defrost them then roughly chop them (no need to pit them). Stew the cherries in the cold water until soft. Force the cherries through a sieve using a wooden spoon to remove the skins and stones.

Put the cherries and sugar into a saucepan over medium heat, stirring frequently. When it starts to boil, add the orange juice. Keep simmering until the liquid is reduced by one third, stirring occasionally.

Mix the cornstarch with a splash of water and slowly add to the cherry mixture. When it thickens (about 5 minutes), ladle into the sterilized jars and leave to set, then cover and refrigerate.

REDCURRANT JELLY

Makes approx. 2 cups (550 g)

These are more than a nice garnish—currants make a tart and beautifully colored jelly that is great with poultry and pork. Look for them in farmers' markets in early summer or grow your own.

> 2 lb (900 g) redcurrants
> Generous 3 cups (750 ml) water
> Sugar (amount depends on the yield of juice)

Wash the fruit (you can get away with not removing the stalks). Put in a soup pot with the water and simmer for 30 minutes over low heat. When the fruit is tender, mash it well using a potato masher and leave it to cool slightly.

Strain the fruit though a scalded jelly bag into a large bowl or pot and leave it overnight to drip.

The next day wash some half-pint jam jars in hot soapy water then sterilize them (see page 57).

Measure the juice and use 2 lb (900 g) sugar per 5¼ cups (1.25 liters) of redcurrant juice. Add the appropriate amount of sugar to the juice in the large pot and heat slowly over low heat to dissolve the sugar.

Once the sugar is dissolved, bring to a rapid boil and let it bubble until it reaches setting point. To test that it is set, place a small spoonful of the jelly on a chilled saucer. Let it sit for a few minutes then draw your finger across it. If it leaves a wrinkle and the jelly doesn't flow back together again then it is set. If it has not set, continue to boil for another few minutes then do another test. At setting point, turn off the heat and ladle the jelly into your hot jars.

Allow to cool and then cover and store in the refrigerator. Or for pantry storage, use the boiling water method of canning: Wipe the rims of your hot jars of jelly with a clean cloth, and top them with two-piece lids screwed on finger-tight. Place in a pot of hot water deep enough to cover the tops by 1 inch, and bring to a boil. Continue to boil for 10 minutes. Allow to sit for 5 more minutes before removing jars carefully to a location where they can set for at least 12 hours before you check the seals and store in your pantry. (For more information on safe canning and preserving, see the website of the The National Center for Home Food Preservation. https://nchfp.uga.edu/publications/publications_usda.html).

BELTANE BANNOCK

Serves 2 to 4

It is good luck to eat a Beltane bannock on Beltane morning, and if you do so it is said your crops will do well (hopefully this means my vegetable patch!). This oatmeal bannock would have been originally made from bacon fat, but butter will do perfectly well. It would have been cooked on a griddle on top of the fire too, but we can use the oven! I love oatmeal bannocks with butter and honey for breakfast.

> ½ cup (50 g) self-rising flour
> 1 cup (150 g) fine oatmeal, plus extra for dusting
> A pinch of baking soda
> ½ teaspoon salt
> 3½ tablespoons (50 g) butter
> Warm water, to mix

Sift the flour into a bowl then mix in the rest of the dry ingredients. Rub the butter into the dry ingredients with your fingers until it resembles fine breadcrumbs. Mix in just enough warm water to make a stiff dough. Working quickly, divide the dough into two pieces.

Sprinkle your work surface with oatmeal and work each piece of dough into a round. Roll out and score into sections.

Cook on a buttered griddle or heavy-based, nonstick frying pan over medium-high heat for 5 minutes on one side. Then flip and finish cooking the bannocks under the broiler for another 5 minutes. Alternatively, preheat the oven to 300°F (150°C), place the bannocks on a greased baking sheet, and bake for 45 minutes.

LITHA

Each day that comes, my strength doth grow.
Oh Lord and Lady I've come to know,
You hear my prayers and answer me,
Your love and bounty sets me free.
This Litha day your power and grace
They purify and bless this place.
Accept these gifts I leave for you,
My love, as ever, always true.

CHAPTER SEVEN

LITHA

OR MIDSUMMER, SUMMER SOLSTICE (JUNE 21ST)

This is a happy time when the God and Goddess are at the peak of their power and the sun is at the highest point. Midsummer is a beautiful time and romance and love are still in the air, but we must think of the days gone by and those that are still to come because at this point, we are halfway through the summer and moving towards the autumn, with winter to follow. At this time, I am usually picking and drying the first of the edible flower heads and storing them for teas, remedies, and ritual or spell work.

LITHA COLORS

Colors associated with Litha are green, white, blue, and yellow.

LITHA CRYSTALS

Crystals associated with Litha are malachite, lapis, sodalite, and citrine.

LITHA INCENSE

Incense for Litha can be made by using dried chamomile, gardenia, lavender, and rose petals. To any of these base ingredients you can add various gums or resins, such as gum Arabic or myrrh resin. Put your mixture into a small jar and label accordingly. This mixture can be sprinkled over charcoal disks.

LITHA PURPOSE

This is a time of purification and empowerment. The sun is high in the sky and plant life is growing well, but from this day we start to move towards winter so we must remember to give thanks for the fruits of the earth that we have been blessed with. One way of showing gratitude is to leave an offering plate outside with some summer fruits and tasty bits for the birds and bees and summer fairies.

As with all rituals or ceremonies in the following pages, please feel free to amend them to suit your own needs, preferences, or purposes.

LITHA RITUAL

Please refer to the instructions on page 41 (Samhain Ritual) to set up your circle. Then say these words or create your own:

> *The circle is about to be cast.*
> *Let none be here but of their own free will.*

Pick up your matches and move to the east and light the east candle saying:

> *Here do I bring into the east light and air to illuminate this circle and bring it the breath of life.*

The south candle is lit saying:

> *Here do I bring into the south light and fire to illuminate this circle and bring it warmth.*

The west candle is lit saying:

> *Here do I bring into the west light and water to illuminate this circle and wash it clean.*

The north candle is lit saying:

> *Here do I bring into the north light and earth to illuminate this circle and build it in strength.*

Return to your altar and say:

> *This circle line I now prepare,*
> *Let no one enter should they dare.*
> *This sacred space I dedicate,*
> *Filled with love and never hate.*
> *So mote it be.*

Pick up your athame or wand or use the index finger of your dominant hand and draw the circle in the air, starting at the east, reaching the south, the west, then the north, and back to the east. Next touch the salt on your altar with your athame, wand, or index finger and say:

> *As salt is life, let it purify me so that I may use it to cleanse my body and spirit in honor of the God and Goddess.*

Put three pinches of salt in the water dish then raise your hand high, pointing your athame, wand, or index finger upwards, feeling the energy flowing into your arm. Put your athame, wand, or index finger into the water and stir three times, saying:

Salt is life, here is life, blessed be without strife, salt is life, here is life, blessed be without strife, salt is life, here is life, sacred be without strife.

Sprinkle the salted water around the circle edge starting at the east, moving to the south, the west, then the north, and back to the east. Return to your altar and put down the consecrated water. Light any altar candles and your incense then pick up the athame, wand, or use your index finger to call the elemental guardians by drawing pentacles in the air, saying:

With air, fire, water, and earth I purify and charge you, east, hail guardians of the watchtower of the east, I invoke you [insert the name of the God or Goddess of your choice], come by the air that is your breath, may you stand in strength ever watching over this circle.

With fire, water, earth, and air I purify and charge you, south, hail guardians of the watchtower of the south, I invoke you [insert the name of the God or Goddess of your choice], come by the fire that is your spirit, may you stand in strength ever watching over this circle.

With water, earth, air, and fire I purify and charge you, west, hail guardians of the watchtower of the west, I invoke you [insert the name of the God or Goddess of your choice], come by the waters of your earthy womb that give us life, may you stand in strength ever watching over this circle.

With earth, air, fire, and water, I purify and charge you, north, hail guardians of the watchtower of the north, I invoke you [insert the name of the God or Goddess of your choice], come by the earth that is your body, may you stand in strength ever watching over this circle.

Take a drink from the chalice and focus your mind on the God and the Goddess. Then, standing in the Goddess position with your arms held high, invoke the Goddess energy into yourself and say:

Lady you have been known by many. I worship and adore you and invite you to join me in body and spirit. Be with me and guide me in the true ways.

Pick up your athame or wand or use your index finger and draw a pentacle in the air above you and below you and say:

You are here and I thank you for the gifts that you have given. I know that you only help those who help themselves. I say:

Each day that comes, my strength doth grow.
My Lord and Lady I've come to know.
You hear my prayers and answer me,
Your love and bounty sets me free.
This Litha day your power and grace
It purifies and blesses this place.
Accept these gifts I leave for you,
My love, as ever, always true.
An it harm none, do what thou will.
What we send forth will return thrice over, so we send it forth with light and love.
So mote it be.

Visualize your prayers and wishes rising to the moon Goddess. Pick up the chalice or cup in your left hand and the athame or wand in your right hand and hold them at eye level then place the point of the athame or wand or your index finger into the wine and say:

May male and female be joined and let all be fruitful throughout the land. The food I eat is the blessing of the Gods and I remember those who have none. I am grateful for all I have been given and am open and ready to receive that which is still to come.
So mote it be.

We have met in love and friendship, let us part the same way, spreading the love from this circle outward to all, sharing it with those we meet. Lord and Lady my thanks to you for sharing this time with me, guarding and guiding me.
Merry we meet, merry we part, merry we meet again.
The circle will now be closed.

Finish with:

Take for your use, eastern watchtower, any powers of air that have not been used.
Take for your use, southern watchtower, any powers of fire that have not been used.
Take for your use, western watchtower, any powers of water that have not been used.
Take for your use, northern watchtower, any powers of earth that have not been used.
The circle is now closed but the work continues.
Let it harm none, so mote it be.

LITHA FOODS

Vegetables such as lettuce, runner beans, and shallots; fruits such as strawberries, raspberries, apples, tomatoes, and plums; and grains of all kinds. Chicken, fish, fresh salads, and any seasonal foods are acceptable. Traditional drinks are ales, mead, and fresh fruit juices of any kind.

LITHA RECIPES

CREAM OF TOMATO SOUP

Serves 4

> 2–3 lb (1–1.5 kg) tomatoes
> 1 tablespoon tomato paste
> Water or vegetable stock
> A good handful of fresh herbs, such as parsley, basil, or oregano
> Salt and freshly ground black pepper
> Cream, to serve

Place your tomatoes into a large pot of boiling water and leave them until the skins have split, then drain the water. Remove the skins and the hard core from the center of the tomatoes and return to a new pot over high heat with the tomato paste and just enough water or stock to cover. Bring to a boil then reduce the heat to low and simmer for 20 minutes.

Remove from the heat and set aside to cool for 20 minutes. Using a blender, food processor, or hand-held immersion blender, purée the tomatoes and fresh herbs until very smooth. Return to the pot and season with salt and pepper to taste. Bring back to a boil and then remove from the heat. Swirl some cream over the top and serve immediately.

CHICKEN GOUJONS

Serves 2

Oil, for frying
1 egg
½ cup (60 g) all-purpose flour
1 cup (240 ml) water or cold stock
A good pinch of salt and freshly ground black pepper
2 medium chicken breasts, cut into strips

To serve (optional)
Side salad
French fries
Mayonnaise (page 33), seasoned to your liking
Finely chopped herbs to suit your ritual work

If deep-frying, preheat the oil in a deep-fryer until it reachs 400°F (200°C). To test the temperature without a thermometer, drop a small piece of bread into the hot oil. When ready, the bread will immediately rise to the surface and begin to turn a nice golden brown.

Meanwhile, beat the egg in a bowl and set aside. Put a ½ cup (60 g) of the flour on a plate and set aside. Place the remaining flour in a bowl with the salt and pepper and mix well, before gradually stirring in enough cold stock or water to create a light and runny batter.

Dip each strip of chicken into the egg, then into the flour, then into the batter to coat well, then set aside.

If deep-frying, carefully place the chicken pieces into the deep-fryer. When cooked through, they will float to the surface and be golden brown, about 5 minutes. Alternatively, to shallow-fry, line a heavy based frying pan with enough oil to coat the bottom and fry the chicken pieces, turning them so they are cooked through and golden on both sides. You may need to work in batches.

Serve with a salad, french fries, seasoned mayonnaise for dipping, and finely chopped herbs suitable for your spell work or ritual.

CHICKEN KORMA

Serves 2 to 3

It is commonly supposed that korma is a mild curry. That is really not the case—you can make it as hot as you want it to be. And if you want it hot, why not add a chopped fresh green chili?

Purée Base

1 large onion, peeled and quartered

1 teaspoon turmeric

4 tablespoons olive oil

3 small tomatoes, halved

1 small green pepper, coarsely chopped

¼ oz (10 g) fresh ginger, coarsely chopped

1 garlic clove, chopped

1 teaspoon fresh cilantro, chopped

1 cup (240 ml) warm water

A pinch of salt

Chicken

7 tablespoons vegetable oil

3 or 4 green cardamom pods

2 bay leaves

1 large onion, finely sliced

4 teaspoons Garam Masala (page 45)

1 lb (450 g) boneless chicken, cut into small cubes

¼ cup (60 ml) warm water (or more, if needed)

Generous ⅓ cup (90 ml) coconut milk

4–5 teaspoons sugar

⅔ cups (150 ml) light cream, plus extra to serve

2 pats of butter or ghee

First make the purée: Place the oil in a frying pan set over low heat and fry the onion and turmeric gently until softened. In a saucepan, combine the tomatoes, pepper, ginger, garlic, and cilantro, water, and salt. Cover and simmer over medium-low heat for about 10 minutes, stirring occasionally, until the vegetables are soft. Add the onions, then use a blender, food processor, or hand-held immersion blender to purée the vegetables until smooth. Set aside.

For the chicken: Heat the oil in a large soup pot, add the cardamom and bay leaves, and slowly fry them over medium-low heat for 5 minutes. Add the onion and cook until soft and translucent. Add the garam masala and cook for 5 minutes, stirring continuously. Add the purée you just made and cook for further 3–4 minutes, stirring occasionally. Add the chicken and water, bring to a boil, and cook for 3–4 minutes. Reduce the heat and simmer for 30 minutes, stirring occasionally.

Add the coconut milk, sugar, and cream, return to a boil, then turn down the heat and simmer for a further 10–15 minutes until slightly thickened. Lastly, add the butter or ghee, stir everything together, and then leave the curry to settle for 10–15 minutes over low heat until it reaches your desired consistency. Before serving, garnish with a little extra cream on top.

WHITE FISH GOUJONS

Serves 4

Oil, for frying
4 medium fillets of firm white fish,
    sliced diagonally into pieces
1 egg
1¼ cups (180 g) all-purpose flour
Salt and freshly ground black pepper
2½ cups (600 ml) water or beer

To serve (optional)
Side salad
French fries
Mayonnaise (page 33), seasoned to your liking
Green Beans with Rice and Tomato (page 187)
Finely chopped herbs to suit your ritual work

If deep-frying, preheat the oil in a deep-fryer until it reachs 400°F (200°C). To test the temperature without a thermometer, drop a small piece of bread into the hot oil. When ready, the bread will immediately rise to the surface and begin to turn a nice golden brown.

Meanwhile, beat the egg in a bowl and set aside. Put a ½ cup (60 g) of the flour on a plate and set aside. Place the remaining flour in a bowl with the salt and pepper and mix well, before gradually stirring in enough cold stock or water to create a light and runny batter.

Dip each strip of fish into the egg, then into the flour, then into the batter to coat well, then set aside.

If deep-frying, carefully place the fish pieces into the deep-fryer. When cooked through, they will float to the surface and be golden brown, about 5 minutes. Alternatively, to shallow-fry, line a heavy based frying pan with enough oil to coat the bottom and fry the fish pieces, turning them so they are cooked through and golden on both sides. You may need to work in batches.

Serve with a salad, french fries, seasoned mayonnaise for dipping, Green Beans with Rice and Tomato, and finely chopped herbs suitable for your spell work or ritual.

Spaghetti Carbonara

Serves 4

14 oz (350 g) spaghetti
6 oz (180 g) bacon, diced
2 egg yolks
⅔ cup (60 g) Parmesan or pecorino cheese, finely grated
½ cup (125 ml) light cream
Salt and freshly ground black pepper

Cook the spaghetti as directed on the package. While the spaghetti is cooking, fry the bacon until it is crispy then set aside. In a bowl, mix together the egg yolks, cheese, and cream. When the spaghetti is cooked, drain immediately and return it to the pot over low heat, quickly add the egg, cheese, and cream mixture, and stir thoroughly. Add the bacon and season to taste (I recommend extra black pepper), stir well, and serve immediately.

Tomato Salad with Onion

Serves 4

1 onion, finely sliced
6 tomatoes, coarsely chopped
2 garlic cloves, chopped or crushed
Juice from 1 whole lemon (you will need to measure the amount)
Same quantity of olive oil as lemon juice
Pinch of salt and freshly ground black pepper
Crusty bread, for serving
Cold smoked mackerel or tuna fish, for serving (optional)

Place the onion, tomatoes, garlic, and salt and pepper in a salad a bowl and thoroughly mix. Whisk the lemon juice and olive oil together then pour into the bowl and stir everything together. Chill for at least 1 hour before serving.

Serve with crusty bread for dipping into the juices at the bottom of the bowl. This is also delicious served with cold smoked mackerel or tuna fish.

DANDELION SALAD

Serves 4

This salad is really easy to make and can be served alongside other salads. Dandelion leaves are useful for disease prevention because they have powerful antioxidant properties. With the combination of dandelion leaves and basil, a serving of this dish would be ideal to follow a ritual for protection, especially with regard to health. Do not gather the leaves from the side of the road because they may be polluted by traffic fumes, but rather look in a country field or a garden.

> 2 loosely packed cups (100 g) dandelion leaves, washed
> 1 red onion, finely sliced
> 6 cherry tomatoes, chopped
> A few fresh basil leaves, sliced, or 1 teaspoon dried basil
> Olive oil, for drizzling
> Salt and freshly ground black pepper

Combine the dandelion leaves, onion, tomatoes, and basil in a salad bowl, drizzle with olive oil, and season to taste. Serve on its own or as an accompaniment to other dishes.

Green Beans with Rice and Tomato

Serves 4

    1 tablespoon extra virgin olive oil
    6 oz (180 g) runner beans, or other green beans, fresh or frozen,
        cut into 1-inch (2.5 cm) pieces
    2 garlic cloves, crushed
    2 tablespoons tomato paste
    Perfect Rice, to serve (page 35, made from 1 cup/200 g rice)
    A handful of freshly chopped herbs (your preference), to garnish
    Garlic Bread (page 215), to serve (optional)

Heat the olive oil in a frying pan over medium heat, add the beans and garlic, and cook for 10 minutes. Add the tomato paste and mix thoroughly. If the purée is too thick or does not cover all the beans, add a little water until you reach your desired consistency, then heat through. You are looking for a nice creamy coating over all the beans.

Serve on top of the Perfect Rice and garnish with the fresh herbs. Alternatively, you could stir the herbs into the beans, then serve with Garlic Bread for dipping.

Roasted Peppers

    1 large or 2 small peppers per person, halved,
        seeds, stalk, and core removed
    Olive oil, for drizzling
    Salt and freshly ground black pepper

Preheat the oven to 425°F (220°C). Lay the peppers skin side up in a roasting pan, drizzle with olive oil, and season to taste. Bake for 15–20 minutes, or until the skins are starting to char. Serve as a side dish.

ROASTED BROCCOLI

Serves 4

> 1 head of broccoli, cut into florets (you can save any
> nice outer leaves for a soup stock)
> 1 tablespoon olive oil
> 3–4 garlic cloves, finely chopped
> A dash of lemon juice, to serve (optional)

Preheat the oven to 400°F (200°C). Place the florets in a large bowl, add the olive oil, and use your fingers to mix until the broccoli is evenly coated in the oil. Dump the florets onto a baking sheet and sprinkle with the garlic. Bake in the oven until the florets are browned on the outside, about 15 minutes. Eat the broccoli on its own with a dash of lemon juice or serve with any roast dish.

BANANA PANCAKES

Serves 3

Bananas are high in potassium, which is essential for healthy function of the nervous system and the muscles. But who's thinking about that when faced with a delicious syrupy treat!

> 1 quantity Pancakes (page 36)
> ¾ cup (170 g) butter
> ¾ cup (180 ml) golden or maple syrup
> 3 large bananas, sliced

Melt the butter in a large, deep frying pan over low heat, add the syrup, and stir well. Add the sliced bananas and, using a spoon or spatula, gently mix to ensure the bananas are well coated. Once the fruit begins to soften, add the cooked pancakes to the pan and cover with the fruit, allowing the pancakes to absorb the syrup. Serve immediately.

BREAD AND BUTTER PUDDING WITH APPLES

Serves 4

9 tablespoons (125 g) butter, plus a little extra for the topping

6–8 slices of white bread

3 red apples, cleaned, cored, and sliced (you can reserve
the seeds to plant for spell work)

A handful of dried fruits

Scant ⅔ cup (125 g) sugar

1 egg, beaten

Scant 1¼ cup (285 ml) whole milk, plus extra if needed

1 teaspoon cinnamon

A pinch of grated nutmeg

Whipped cream, for serving

Preheat the oven to 350°F (180°C). Butter the slices of bread and layer one-third of the bread slices across the bottom of a 2-inch (5 cm) deep baking dish. Place half of the apple slices on top of the bread and sprinkle with half of the dried fruit and half of the sugar. Place another layer of buttered bread over the apples then layer on the remaining apple slices, dried fruit, and sugar on top. Place the last layer of bread slices on top.

Mix the egg, milk, and spices in a bowl then pour over apples and bread. Dot the top layer with butter. If the liquid does not cover the bread completely, add more milk. Bake for 30–40 minutes, or until the bread is golden brown on the top. Serve with whipped cream.

EVE'S PUDDING

Serves 4

This is a hearty, comforting dessert that is like a loose apple cake. It is served hot with whipped cream or Custard (page 32) and generally eaten with a spoon.

2 large cooking apples, peeled, cored, and coarsely chopped
1 tablespoon lemon juice
2 tablespoons (30 ml) water
2 tablespoons (30 g) butter
2 tablespoons sugar

Topping
6 tablespoons (90 g) butter
Scant ⅔ cup (125 g) sugar
Generous 1 cup (125 g) self-rising flour
2 eggs, lightly beaten
1 tablespoon boiling water
Whipped cream or Custard (page 32), to serve

Preheat the oven to 350°F (180°C). Place the apples, lemon juice, and water in a saucepan over medium-high heat, cover with a lid, and cook briskly for 5 minutes until the apples are soft. Add the butter and sugar, stir, then transfer the apples to a 2-inch (5 cm) deep baking dish and set aside to cool.

For the topping, use an electric hand mixer or stand mixer to cream together the butter and sugar until light and fluffy. Fold the flour and egg in alternate spoonfuls into the butter and sugar mixture until blended, being careful to keep folding rather than stirring. Fold in the boiling water, then spoon over the apples.

Bake for 30–35 minutes, or until the topping is puffy and golden. Spoon onto serving dishes and serve with whipped cream or custard.

LITHA CAKE

Serves 4

9 tablespoons (125 g) butter, softened
Scant 1 cup (180 g) dark brown sugar
2 eggs
1 tablespoon lemon juice
Grated zest of 1 lemon
1⅔ cups (180 g) self-rising flour
1 cup (125 g) pecans, crushed

Preheat the oven to 350°F (180°C). Cream the butter and sugar together using an electric hand mixer or stand mixer. Add the eggs, lemon juice, and zest, then mix thoroughly. Fold in the flour and crushed nuts. Bake in a 6-inch (15 cm) cake pan for 30–40 minutes, or until a skewer inserted into the middle comes out clean. Alternatively, line a muffin pan with paper cups and baked as cupcakes at the same temperature for 15–20 minutes, until a skewer inserted into the middle comes out clean.

LITHA PUNCH

Serves 4

1 bottle (750 ml) white wine
2 tablespoons (35 ml) Glayva or other golden-colored spirit or liqueur
Generous 1 cup (250 ml) orange juice (freshly squeezed is best)
A handful of fresh mint
Some seasonal fresh fruit of your choice, finely chopped

Place all the liquids into a large jug and stir well. Add the fresh mint and store in the refrigerator until needed. Add the fresh fruit and ice just before serving.

LITHA MEAD (NON-ALCOHOLIC)

Serves 4

2 whole lemons (unwaxed), one quartered and one juiced

4¼ cups (1 liter) water

1 cup (240 ml) honey

A good pinch of nutmeg, cinnamon, or allspice

Put the quartered lemon in a large pot over high heat with the water, honey, and spices, and bring to a boil. While the liquid is boiling, a foam will rise to the top. This can be carefully removed with a small strainer: run it around the sides of the pot and scoop up the foam. When the foam stops forming, add the lemon juice and set aside to cool before serving.

LEMONADE

Serves 4

1 cup (200 g) sugar

Generous ¾ cup (200 ml) water

Juice of 6 lemons, plus a few slices to serve

Mint leaves, bruised, to serve

Heat the sugar and water in a saucepan until the sugar is dissolved completely. Pour the lemon juice into a large jug or pitcher (4¼ cups/1 liter capacity) then add the sugar syrup and lemon juice. Top up with cold water and ice.

Serve with ice, slices of lemon, and a few mint leaves.

VARIATION: Why not make limeade with fresh limes, brown sugar, plenty of bruised mint leaves, and sparkling mineral or soda water. A bit like a non-alcoholic mojito!

AGUA FRESCA

Serves 4

This is a very refreshing drink for your Litha table. Its Spanish name means "water refreshment." It is an infusion of fresh fruits and vegetable and water. There is no need for added sugar. Serve in a pretty glass jug so that your guests can see the contents, and if they want to eat the bits of fruit then let them! You could also float edible petals on the top of each serving glass to decorate. This should only be kept for a day or two in the refrigerator.

> 1 cucumber, about 2 inches (5 cm) thick, cut into thin slices
> 2–3 strawberries, sliced
> Half of 1 apple, sliced
> 5 mint leaves, chopped
> 4¼ cups (1 liter) cold water
> 1 lemon, one half juiced and one half sliced
> Pot Marigold (calendula) leaves, to garnish (optional)

Add all the ingredients except the lemon and marigold leaves in a large jug or pitcher, then add the lemon juice. Store in the refirgerator to infuse for 1–2 hours. Serve with marigold petals floating in each glass and/or garnish with slices of lemon.

VARIATIONS: There are so many variations you could try based on this recipe, but a few ideas are: melon and orange, fresh ginger and pineapple, or even celery.

MEAD

Serves 4 to 6

Here is one to make at Litha, but you are not going to be able to drink it until next Litha… okay, you can have some at Yule, since it will probably be ready by then! Mead can be flavored with any herbs, spices, and fruits that you prefer. Add these extra ingredients to the carboy (also know as a demijohn). Strain the mixture after it stops fermenting–it has reached this point because the wine airlock will stop bubbling. Bottled, it will keep for a considerable time in a cool, dark place. Read through the recipe entirely before you start.

12½ cups (3 liters) water
7 cups (3 lb) honey
2½ teaspoons wine-making yeast
Herbs, spices, and fruits of your choice for flavoring, chopped

Equipment
1½-gallon (5 liter) carboy with cap, sterilized
A large pot
A funnel
A winemaking airlock (bubbletrap) cork

Bring the water to a boil in a large pot, then cool until it is just warm. Add the honey and yeast.

In the carboy, combine the chopped fruit, spices, and herbs (bruise the leaves first). Using the funnel, pour in a little of the cooled liquid and swirl around to mix. Pour in the rest of the liquid, ensuring there is room for fermentation (frothing) at the top.

Pop in the airlock cork. Pretty soon (within a day or two) you will see the mixture start to ferment—the water in the cork will be bubbling away. It will do this for a good few weeks. Once the mixture is no longer fermenting, strain the liquid and discard any fruits, herbs, or spices that were added, then funnel the liquid back into the carboy and put the cap on it for a few months.

After a few months, bottle and cork it and leave it to age for a further 6 months.

NOTE: This is a traditional method. As always, it is best to consult the USDA food safety website for safe fermentation practices.

LAMMAS

We bake our bread, give thanks and pray,
For the Lammas crops we reap this day.
The Sun God's gifts from fertile earth,
For these good fruits we show our worth.
Oh Mother Earth be fruitful still,
Let future crops our larders fill.
We meet in love and gratitude
For Summer's harvest of good food.

CHAPTER EIGHT

LAMMAS

LUGHNASADH (AUGUST 1ST)

Lammas is the festival of the first harvest, particularly of wheat and corn, and so breads of all kinds are important to Lammas rituals. At this time, the days become shorter and the Sun God's power begins to diminish. Christian churches celebrate the harvest festival and members of the congregation donate breads and produce, and think about metaphorical and spiritual harvests. As pagans, we make corn dolls, bake breads, and give thanks for the foods that we have grown.

LAMMAS COLORS

Colors associated with Lammas are green, light brown, golden yellow, and orange.

LAMMAS CRYSTALS

Crystals associated with Lammas are aventurine, citrine, peridot, and sardonyx.

LAMMAS INCENSE

Incense can be made using dried thyme, marjoram, rose, and sandalwood. To any of these base ingredients you can add various gums or resins, such as gum Arabic or myrrh resin. Put your mixture into a small jar and label accordingly. This mixture can be sprinkled over charcoal disks.

LAMMAS PURPOSE

The farmers are beginning to harvest their crops and preparing to store them for the coming winter months. This is a time of abundance and we should give thanks for the gifts that we have received by leaving offerings to the four quarters.

As with all rituals or ceremonies in the following pages, please feel free to amend them to suit your own needs, preferences, or purposes.

LAMMAS RITUAL

Please refer to the instructions on page 41 (Samhain Ritual) to set up your circle. Then say these words or create your own:

> *The circle is about to be cast.*
> *Let none be here but of their own free will.*

Pick up your matches and move to the east and light the east candle saying:

> *Here do I bring into the east light and air to illuminate this circle and bring it the breath of life.*

The south candle is lit saying:

> *Here do I bring into the south light and fire to illuminate this circle and bring it warmth.*

The west candle is lit saying:

> *Here do I bring into the west light and water to illuminate this circle and wash it clean.*

The north candle is lit saying:

> *Here do I bring into the north light and earth to illuminate this circle and build it in strength.*

Return to your altar and say:

> *This circle line I now prepare,*
> *Let no one enter should they dare.*
> *This sacred space I dedicate,*
> *Filled with love and never hate.*
> *So mote it be.*

Pick up your athame or wand or use the index finger of your dominant hand and draw the circle in the air, starting at the east, reaching the south, the west, then the north, and back to the east. Next touch the salt on your altar with your athame, wand, or index finger and say:

> *As salt is life, let it purify me so that I may use it to cleanse my body and spirit in honor of the God and Goddess.*

Put three pinches of salt in the water dish then raise your hand high, pointing your athame, wand, or index finger upwards, feeling the energy flowing into your arm. Put your athame, wand, or index finger into the water and stir three times, saying:

> *Salt is life, here is life, blessed be without strife, salt is life, here is life, blessed be without strife, salt is life, here is life, sacred be without strife.*

Sprinkle the salted water round the circle edge starting at the east, moving to the south, the west, then the north, and back to the east. Return to your altar and put down the consecrated water. Light any altar candles and your incense then pick up the athame, wand, or use your index finger to call the elemental guardians by drawing pentacles in the air, saying:

> *With air, fire, water, and earth I purify and charge you, east, hail guardians of the watchtower of the east, I invoke you [insert the name of the God or Goddess of your choice], come by the air that is your breath, may you stand in strength ever watching over this circle.*

> *With fire, water, earth, and air I purify and charge you, south, hail guardians of the watchtower of the south, I invoke you [insert the name of the God or Goddess of your choice], come by the fire that is your spirit, may you stand in strength ever watching over this circle.*

> *With water, earth, air, and fire I purify and charge you, west, hail guardians of the watchtower of the west, I invoke you [insert the name of the God or Goddess of your choice], come by the waters of your earthy womb that give us life, may you stand in strength ever watching over this circle.*

> *With earth, air, fire, and water, I purify and charge you, north, hail guardians of the watchtower of the north, I invoke you [insert the name of the God or Goddess of your choice], come by the earth that is your body, may you stand in strength ever watching over this circle.*

Take a drink from the chalice and focus your mind on the God and the Goddess. Then, standing in the Goddess position with your arms held high, invoke the Goddess energy into yourself and say:

> *Lady you have been known by many. I worship and adore you and invite you to join me in body and spirit. Be with me and guide me in the true ways.*

Pick up your athame or wand or use your index finger and draw a pentacle in the air above you and below you and say:

> *You are here and I thank you for the gifts that you have given. I know that you only help those who help themselves. I say:*

> *We bake our bread, give thanks and pray,*

For the Lammas crops we reap this day.
The Sun God's gifts from fertile earth.
For these good fruits we show our worth.
Oh Mother Earth be fruitful still,
Let future crops our larders fill.
We meet in love and gratitude
For Summer's harvest of good food.
An it harm none, do what thou will.
What we send forth will return thrice over, so we send it forth with light and love.
So mote it be.

Visualize your prayers and wishes rising to the moon Goddess. Pick up the chalice or cup in your left hand and the athame or wand in your right hand and hold them at eye level then place the point of the athame or wand or your index finger into the wine and say:

May male and female be joined and let all be fruitful throughout the land. The food I eat is the blessing of the Gods and I remember those who have none. I am grateful for all I have been given and am open and ready to receive that which is still to come.
So mote it be.

We have met in love and friendship, let us part the same way, spreading the love from this circle outward to all, sharing it with those we meet. Lord and Lady my thanks to you for sharing this time with me, guarding and guiding me.
Merry we meet, merry we part, merry we meet again.
The circle will now be closed.

Finish with:

Take for your use, eastern watchtower, any powers of air that have not been used.
Take for your use, southern watchtower, any powers of fire that have not been used.
Take for your use, western watchtower, any powers of water that have not been used.
Take for your use, northern watchtower, any powers of earth that have not been used.
The circle is now closed but the work continues.
Let it harm none, so mote it be.

LAMMAS FOODS

Foods appropriate for Lammas are breads using wholewheat, granary, and white flours, as well as foods containing berries. Rice, barley, nuts, and seasonal fruits and vegetables are also favored.

LAMMAS RECIPES

SPAGHETTI BOLOGNESE

Serves 4

From time to time, I add a handful of corn kernels and/or a stick of celery during the cooking process (remove the celery before serving). Finely sliced mushrooms also make a nice addition. You could also vary it by using a mixture of half ground beef and half ground pork. Spaghetti is traditional, but this is a lovely sauce to serve with almost every kind of pasta.

14 oz (350 g) spaghetti
Salt

Bolognese Sauce
1 lb (450 g) ground beef
1 tablespoon olive oil
1 onion, finely chopped
4 garlic cloves, finely chopped
A handful of fresh oregano leaves, or 1 tablespoon dried (if using
    fresh, add at the end; if using dried, add at the beginning)
14 oz (400 g) can whole tomatoes, peeled and chopped, or 8 fresh
    tomatoes, skinned, cored, and chopped
3 tablespoons tomato paste
1 tablespoon Parmesan cheese, grated
Salt and freshly ground black pepper
Garlic Bread (page 215) or Ciabatta Bread (page 213), to serve

Place the beef into a nonstick large pot over low heat and brown it thoroughly in its own fat, breaking it up with a wooden spatula as you go.

While your beef is cooking, heat the olive oil in a sauté pan over low heat then add the onion and cook until soft and translucent, about 10 minutes. (My secret to a really good bolognese sauce is to slightly brown the onions, but only after they are soft.) Add the garlic and cook gently for 5 minutes. If you are using dried oregano, add it at this point.

Add the contents of the sauté pan to the pot with the beef, then add the tomatoes, tomato paste, and Parmesan. Stir everything together and add enough water to just cover the sauce. Bring to a boil then simmer for at least 1–1½ hours (the longer it simmers, the more the flavors will develop).

About 10 minutes before you are ready to serve, cook the spaghetti in boiling salted water as instructed on the package. When it is ready, drain it.

If you are using fresh oregano, add it to the sauce now and season to taste before serving over the pasta. Serve with Garlic Bread or Ciabatta.

BIRYANI

Serves 6

Various meats and/or vegetables can be used when making curries of any kind, including this curried rice dish. Just vary the recipe to suit your requirements or spell working.

6 medium boneless chicken breasts

½ cup (125 g) plain yogurt

8 tablespoons sunflower oil

3 large onions, 2 finely chopped and 1 finely sliced

1-inch (2.5 cm) piece of fresh ginger, peeled and finely chopped

2 garlic cloves, finely chopped

2 large green chilies, finely sliced

1 tablespoon coriander seeds, crushed

2 teaspoons cumin seeds, crushed

Generous ¾ cups (250 g) basmati rice

2 oz (60 g) raisins

Pinch of saffron, soaked in a little boiling water

Scant 1¼ cups (285 ml) chicken stock

1 oz (30 g) whole almonds

Salt and freshly ground black pepper

Place the chicken breasts in a shallow dish and cover with the yogurt, cover with a lid or plastic wrap, and leave to marinate in the refrigerator for a minimum of 3 hours (or overnight).

Heat 3 tablespoons of the oil in a large, heavy-based frying pan (use one that has a lid) over medium-high heat and fry the chopped onion, ginger, garlic, and half of the chilies (reserving the rest for garnish) until golden, 5 minutes. Add the coriander and cumin, and season to taste. Stir in the rice and raisins then pour in the saffron water and chicken stock. Cover, reduce the heat to low, and simmer for 12–15 minutes, until the rice is tender but still a little firm. Do not mix it.

Remove the chicken from the yogurt and discard the yogurt. Lightly salt the chicken. Heat another 3 tablespoons of the remaining oil in a large frying pan and brown the chicken breasts for 2–3 minutes on each side. Add to the rice mixture and simmer for an additional 5–10 minutes, until the chicken is cooked through and piping hot.

In a separate frying pan, heat the remaining 2 tablespoons of oil over medium-high heat and fry the finely sliced onion until golden and crisp, about 5 minutes. Stir in the almonds, then drain the mixture on paper towels. Serve on top of the biryani and top with the remaining sliced chilies.

Minestrone Soup

Serves 6 to 8

2 tablespoons olive oil

1 onion, finely chopped

1 garlic bulb, peeled and finely chopped or crushed

Two 14-oz (400 g) cans chopped tomatoes, or 2 lb (900 g) fresh
    tomatoes, skinned and chopped (see page 180 for my method)

4¼ cups (1 liter) ham stock (page 25)

2 carrots, grated

½ head white cabbage, cut into bite-sized chunks

1 celery stick (or more, if you like), finely sliced

1 smoked sausage (any variety), finely sliced

3 tablespoons tomato paste

⅔ cup (60 g) Parmesan cheese, finely grated

Salt and freshly ground black pepper

Heat the olive oil in a large soup pot over low heat then add the onion and cook very slowly until soft and translucent, about 10 minutes. Add the garlic, tomatoes, and stock and bring to a boil. Add the carrots, cabbage, celery, and smoked sausage to the pot and give everything a good stir. Add the tomato paste and Parmesan, stir, then reduce the heat to medium and simmer until some of the liquid has evaporated and the soup has a chunky consistency, about 20 minutes. If it becomes too thick, you can add some more stock or water to reach your desired consistency. Before serving, taste and adjusting the seasoning as needed.

NOTE: Canned tomatoes and tomato paste can sometimes be a little bitter. Taste your soup before serving and add 1 teaspoon sugar if needed.

CHICKEN WITH TARRAGON

Serves 2

Tarragon helps to stimulate the appetite and was traditionally claimed to cure toothaches. This goes well with Creamy Potatoes with Nutmeg (page 207) and Roasted Roots (page 209).

    1 tablespoon olive oil
    1 small onion, finely chopped
    2 medium chicken breasts
    ¼ cup (30 g) all-purpose flour
    A pat of butter
    1 cup (240 ml) heavy cream
    Fresh or dried tarragon (as much as you wish)

Heat the olive oil in a frying pan over medium heat. Add the onion and gently fry until it is transparent but not brown. When it is cooked, remove from the pan and set aside.

Put the flour on a plate. Rinse the chicken in cold water then dip into the flour so that both sides are coated.

Melt the butter in the same frying pan over medium heat then gently place the chicken breasts in the pan and fry slowly, for 3–4 minutes per side, until browned and cooked through. Add the onion, cream, and tarragon, heat through, and serve.

CREAMY POTATOES WITH NUTMEG   *Serves 4 to 6*

3 lb (1.5 kg) potatoes, peeled and cut into
    ½-inch (1 cm) thick slices
A good pinch of salt and freshly ground black pepper
A good pinch of freshly grated nutmeg
4 tablespoons (60 g) butter, diced
1 tablespoon heavy cream

Preheat the oven to 350°F (180°C). Arrange the potatoes in the base of a pie dish. Add the salt and pepper and nutmeg. Dot the tops of the potatoes with the butter then bake for 40 minutes.

Remove the dish from the oven and check that the potatoes are done—pierce a few slices with a knife to make sure they are soft and heated through. Add the cream and another pinch of nutmeg. Return to the oven and bake for another 10 minutes. Serve immediately.

MUSTARD MASH   *Serves 4 to 6*

3 lb (1.5 kg) potatoes, peeled and quartered
4 tablespoons (60 g) butter
2 tablespoons whole-grain mustard
Salt and freshly ground black pepper

Put the potatoes in a large pot and cover with water, then bring to a boil and cook for 20–30 minutes, or until they can be pierced easily with a knife. Once they are cooked, drain and transfer them to a bowl (or put back in the pot). Add the butter, season to taste, and thoroughly mash with a potato masher. Stir in the mustard then serve immediately.

STUFFED PEPPERS WITH A CITRUS-YOGURT DRESSING

Serves 4 to 5

Bell peppers are one of the most versatile vegetables and certainly one of my favorites. Simple and easy to use, eat them hot or cold, cooked or raw, on their own or as an accompaniment to other dishes. This vegetarian main dish is fabulous.

Generous ¾ cups (250 g) basmati rice

4–5 bell peppers (any colors; one per person)

4 tablespoons (60 g) butter

1 teaspoon salt

1 teaspoon black pepper

8 oz (250 g) ground beef

4–5 whole garlic cloves (1 per pepper)

Juice of a lemon, to serve

Citrus-Yogurt Dressing

½ cup (120 g) plain yogurt

3 lemons, 1 juiced and 2 quartered

Salt and freshly ground black pepper

Put the rice in a large jug and cover with boiling water. Soak the rice in the water for 5 minutes, stirring it once or twice while you prepare the peppers.

Remove the stalks from the peppers by piercing the top with a sharp knife and scoring around the stalk—you can then pull it out. (Keep the stalks—you will use them during cooking.) As you pull out the stalks, put your fingers into the pepper and remove as much of the pith and seeds as you can. (The seeds can be tossed into a little pot full of compost and left on the kitchen window to sprout.)

Thoroughly drain the rice in a sieve and put it in a bowl. Add the butter, salt, and pepper and, using your hands, mix well until the butter has mostly melted. Add the ground beef and again using your hands, mix well until all the ingredients are thoroughly incorporated.

Loosely fill each pepper almost to the the top with the rice mixture, push in one garlic clove, and put the stalk back on top. Do not press the mixture in too tight because the rice needs to have room to swell.

Arrange the peppers in the bottom of a pot in one layer, pour in water almost to the top of, but not covering, the peppers, and set on high heat. Once boiling, reduce the heat to low and simmer for 40 minutes. Check regularly to make sure that the water does not evaporate (add more as needed).

While the peppers are cooking, make the dressing: Put the yogurt in a jug, add half of the lemon juice and salt and pepper to taste, and stir well.

Remove the peppers from the pot and place them on a serving plate. Drizzle with the remaining lemon juice and the Citrus-Yogurt Dressing and garnish with the lemon quarters.

ROASTED ROOTS
Serves 4 to 6

½ cup (125 ml) olive oil, plus extra for greasing
4 small rutabagas, peeled and diced
4 carrots, peeled and cut into wedges
4 parsnips, peeled and cut in wedges
2 onions, peeled and quartered
A pinch of salt and freshly ground black pepper
(or adjust to suit your taste)

Preheat oven to 350°F (180°C). Grease a small baking tray by pouring a little of the olive oil on it and tipping it around, making sure to coat the entire surface.

Put all the vegetables, remaining olive oil, and salt and pepper in a large bowl. Use your fingers to mix until everything is evenly coated in oil. Dump the vegetables onto the baking tray and bake for 40 minutes, or until the vegetables are browned and crispy around the edges.

EASY STRAWBERRY TARTS

Makes 12

1 portion Shortcrust Pastry (page 28)
1¾ cups (350 g) halved strawberries
A pinch of sugar
A pinch of black pepper
2 tablespoons strawberry jam
2 tablespoons hot water
A few fresh mint leaves, crushed
2½ cups (600 ml) heavy whipping cream

Rest the pastry in the refrigerator for 1 hour. When you are nearing the end of the resting time, put the strawberries in a bowl, sprinkle with the sugar and black pepper, mix well, and set aside in the refrigerator.

Preheat the oven to 350°F (180°C) and grease a 12-hole mini tart pan (or a muffin pan in a pinch) Roll out the shortcrust pastry to a thickness of ⅛ inch (3 mm) and cut into circles using a cutter around 2½ inches (6.5 cm) in diameter, gently re-rolling any offcuts to get approximately 12. Press the circles into the prepared pan and fill each tart base with some pie weights (or just use dried beans or peas). Blind bake for 15 minutes, then remove the pan from the oven and set aside to cool completely.

Put the strawberry jam into a small bowl and stir in the hot water to reduce the thickness of the jam. Add the mint to the thinned jam and stir.

Using an electric hand mixer or stand mixer, whip the cream until it is light and fluffy.

When the pastry is cool, take the strawberries out of the refrigerator and remove the mint leaves from the thinned jam. Spread a little jam into the bottom of each tart, add a spoonful of whipped cream, top with some fresh strawberries, then drizzle with a little more of the thinned jam.

QUICK AND EASY LEMON TARTLETS *Makes 12*

1 portion Shortcrust Pastry (page 28)
10 oz (280 g) jar lemon curd
2½ cups (600 ml) heavy whipping cream

Rest the pastry in the refrigerator for 1 hour.

Preheat the oven to 350°F (180°C). Roll out the pastry to a thickness of ⅛ inch (3 mm) and cut into 12 circles using a 2½ inch (6.5 cm) cookie cutter. Press the circles into a mini tart pan and fill each tart base with some pie weights (or just use dried beans or peas). Blind bake for 15 minutes, then remove the pan from the oven and set aside to cool completely.

Using an electric hand mixer or stand mixer, whip the cream until it is light and fluffy.

When the pastry is cool, spread some lemon curd into the bottom of each pastry case, add a spoonful of whipped cream, then top with a little more of the lemon curd.

ISLAY LOAF

Serves 6 to 8

This loaf is delicious but has to be made in two parts. For best results, make the first part the night before so it will ready for you to finish off in the morning. Believe me, it is worth the effort! Serve spread with a little butter and enjoy it with a nice cup of tea. Mmm, lovely!

Part One
4 tablespoons (60 g) butter
2 cups (300 g) dried fruit, chopped if large
1 cup (200 g) sugar
1 cup (240 ml) water
1 teaspoon baking powder

Part Two
Butter or vegetable oil, for greasing
2 large eggs, beaten
2 cups (220 g) self-rising flour

Place all of the Part One ingredients into a pot over high heat, bring to a boil, then reduce the heat to low and simmer for 15 minutes. Leave to cool completely on the stove, preferably overnight.

The next day, preheat the oven to 350°F (180°C) and grease a 9 x 5 inch (900 g) loaf pan. Add the eggs to the cooled fruit mixture and stir well. Add the flour, thoroughly mix, pour into the prepared pan, and bake for 1 hour, until it sounds hollow when tapped underneath, and your house smells like freshly baked bread.

LAMMAS BREADS

Having once run a boarding house that served fresh bread every day, I became very good at making it. The basic bread recipe on page 30 is a real winner.

Lammas breads are often wholewheat. You can use any of the following breads in your Lamas ritual, formed into shapes that suit your purpose. In some traditions, Lammas bread is formed into the shape of a man to symbolize the harvest god, the Celtic god Lugh.

Pass the bread around before your Lammas feast. Each of your guests can tear off a chunk for their meal. As you pass it around, say a verse of thanks—you could use this or make up your own:

That which dies has new purpose,
Like the harvested grain becoming our bread,
Giving us food for the winter ahead,
The cycle of life leads us all here,
The circle has turned once more this year.
We give thanks for the year's harvest and for the earth's gifts.

If you have wine to share, pass this around too.

CIABATTA BREAD

Makes two 1-lb loaves

2 lb (900 g) white bread flour, plus extra for dusting
2 teaspoons sugar
2 teaspoons salt
2 envelopes (14 g) instant yeast
¼ cup (60 ml) extra virgin olive oil
Generous 1 cup (250 ml) cold water
Generous 1 cup (250 ml) boiling water
Vegetable oil, for greasing

Follow the method on page 30, adding the oil to the dry ingredients before adding the water. Loaf pans are not suitable for this bread; form the proofed dough into your desired shapes and bake on a baking sheet.

WHOLEWHEAT BREAD

Makes one 1–lb loaf

2 lb (900 g) wholewheat bread flour

2 teaspoons sugar

2 teaspoons salt

2 envelopes (14 g) instant yeast

Generous 1 cup (250 ml) cold water

Generous 1 cup (250 ml) boiling water

Follow the bread-making directions on page 30 to make 1 loaf or round.

GRANARY BREAD

Makes one 1–lb loaf

2 lb (900 g) granary flour

2 teaspoons sugar

2 teaspoons salt

2 envelopes (14 g) instant yeast

Generous 1 cup (250 ml) cold water

Generous 1 cup (250 ml) boiling water

Follow the bread-making directions on page 30 to make 1 loaf or round.

GARLIC BREAD WITH OIL AND HERBS

Scant ¾ cup (175 ml) extra virgin olive oil
1 garlic bulb, peeled and either diced or finely crushed
A handful of fresh herbs, chopped (your preference)
1 crusty baguette
Salt and freshly ground black pepper

Preheat the oven to 425°F (220°C) or use your broiler. Pour the olive oil into a shallow baking tray and sprinkle the garlic over the oil. Add the herbs and salt and pepper to taste. Cut the bread into thick slices and dip both sides of each slice in the oil, then transfer to a baking sheet. Bake or broil for 5–10 minutes, until the bread is nicely toasted.

STRAWBERRY JAM
Makes 2–2½ cups (550–650 g)

Could anything be nicer to eat with your Lammas bread than homemade strawberry jam? Make sure that none of the fruit is overripe or bruised. You can easily double this recipe; jut use an equal ratio of sugar to fruit. Strawberries contain very little pectin (the stuff that make jam set to a jelly consistency), so you could add pectin (according to the package instructions) to help it set firmly. I'm not too worried if my strawberry jam is a bit runny because it still tastes delicious!

    8 oz (450 g) strawberries
    8 oz (450 g) sugar
    A pat of butter (omit if processing for longer-term storage)

Wash some jam jars in hot soapy water and then sterilize them (see page 57).

Wash the strawberries and remove any stems. Place the sugar and strawberries in a pot and mix thoroughly. Leave it until the juices from the strawberries start to run.

Once the juices have started to run, turn the heat to low and cook slowly until all the sugar has dissolved, about 20 minutes. Once dissolved, bring the jam to a rolling boil. As it is boiling, it will start to develop a foam on the top—add the butter to remove it, or skim it off with a slotted spoon (do not use butter if processing for longer-term storage). After about 20 minutes, test if it is ready: To test if the jam is set, place a small spoonful on a chilled saucer. Let it sit for a few minutes then draw your finger across the jam. If it leaves a wrinkle and the jam doesn't flow back together again then it is set. If it has not set, continue to boil for another few minutes then do another test.

At setting point, turn off the heat and ladle the jelly into your hot jars. Allow to cool and then cover and store in the refrigerator for up to 1 month. Alternatively, process for longer-term pantry storage according to the instructions on page 171.

MABON

For our blessings we thank the Goddess
And think on those who have much less.
No food on their table, no bed to rest in
No roof to shelter them from rain,
Good health and happiness, good people around them,
No one and nothing to ease their pain.
Let us give to those in need,
With heart and pocket and thought and deed.

CHAPTER NINE

MABON

OR AUTUMN EQUINOX (SEPTEMBER 21ST)

At Mabon, the festival of the autumnal equinox, day and night are equal in length and, as the pagan wheel turns, we see the old Sun God dying. Mother Earth, the Goddess, rests as she carries the fetus of the new Sun God. This is the second harvest and a time to give thanks for the harvest of the year past and think about the coming winter. The nights to come will be long and the days short. The soup pot becomes a standard feature in our kitchens, and we make use of the grains and vegetables that we have grown and stored to last us through the winter.

At this time we should think of others less fortunate than ourselves and donate to needy causes by making financial contributions or in actions.

MABON COLORS

Colors associated with Mabon are brown, orange, violet, maroon, russet, and gold.

MABON CRYSTALS

Crystals associated with Mabon are amethyst, petrified wood, amber, topaz, and citrine.

MABON INCENSE

Incense for Mabon can be made by using frankincense, sandalwood, juniper, pine, oak leaves, and patchouli. To any of these base ingredients you can add various gums or resins, such as gum Arabic or myrrh resin. Put your mixture into a small jar and label accordingly. This mixture can be sprinkled over charcoal disks.

MABON PURPOSE

While we reap the rewards of our harvests, people in other parts of the world are suffering through hardship and poverty. As our winter approaches, we should focus our attention on sending healing energy to those who are suffering through no fault of their own. We should also ask for protection during the coming winter months to ensure that we have enough food and warmth and, more importantly, good health to survive the harsh weather.

As with all rituals or ceremonies in the following pages, please feel free to amend them to suit your own needs, preferences, or purposes.

MABON RITUAL

Please refer to the instructions on page 41 (Samhain Ritual) to set up your circle. Then say these words or create your own:

> The circle is about to be cast.
> Let none be here but of their own free will.

Pick up your matches and move to the east and light the east candle saying:

> Here do I bring into the east light and air to illuminate this circle and bring it the breath of life.

The south candle is lit saying:

> Here do I bring into the south light and fire to illuminate this circle and bring it warmth.

The west candle is lit saying:

> Here do I bring into the west light and water to illuminate this circle and wash it clean.

The north candle is lit saying:

> Here do I bring into the north light and earth to illuminate this circle and build it in strength.

Return to your altar and say:

> This circle line I now prepare,
> Let no one enter should they dare.
> This sacred space I dedicate,
> Filled with love and never hate.
> So mote it be.

Pick up your athame or wand or use the index finger of your dominant hand and draw the circle in the air, starting at the east, reaching the south, the west, then the north, and back to the east. Next touch the salt on your altar with your athame, wand, or index finger and say:

As salt is life, let it purify me so that I may use it to cleanse my body and spirit in honor of the God and Goddess.

Put three pinches of salt in the water dish then raise your hand high, pointing your athame, wand, or index finger upwards, feeling the energy flowing into your arm. Put your athame, wand, or index finger into the water and stir three times, saying:

Salt is life, here is life, blessed be without strife, salt is life, here is life, blessed be without strife, salt is life, here is life, sacred be without strife.

Sprinkle the salted water round the circle edge starting at the east, moving to the south, the west, then the north, and back to the east. Return to your altar and put down the consecrated water. Light any altar candles and your incense then pick up the athame, wand, or use your index finger to call the elemental guardians by drawing pentacles in the air, saying:

With air, fire, water, and earth I purify and charge you, east, hail guardians of the watchtower of the east, I invoke you [insert the name of the God or Goddess of your choice], come by the air that is your breath, may you stand in strength ever watching over this circle.

With fire, water, earth, and air I purify and charge you, south, hail guardians of the watchtower of the south, I invoke you [insert the name of the God or Goddess of your choice], come by the fire that is your spirit, may you stand in strength ever watching over this circle.

With water, earth, air, and fire I purify and charge you, west, hail guardians of the watchtower of the west, I invoke you [insert the name of the God or Goddess of your choice], come by the waters of your earthy womb that give us life, may you stand in strength ever watching over this circle.

With earth, air, fire, and water, I purify and charge you, north, hail guardians of the watchtower of the north, I invoke you [insert the name of the God or Goddess of your choice], come by the earth that is your body, may you stand in strength ever watching over this circle.

Take a drink from the chalice and focus your mind on the God and the Goddess. Then, standing in the Goddess position with your arms held high, invoke the Goddess energy into yourself and say:

Lady you have been known by many. I worship and adore you and invite you to join me in body and spirit. Be with me and guide me in the true ways.

Pick up your athame or wand or use your index finger and draw a pentacle in the air above you and below you and say:

> You are here and I thank you for the gifts that you have given. I know that you only help those who help themselves. I say:

> For our blessings we thank the Goddess
> And think on those who have much less.
> No food on their table, no bed to rest in,
> No roof to shelter them from rain,
> Good health and happiness, good people around them.
> No one and nothing to ease their pain.
> Let us give to those in need,
> With heart and pocket and thought and deed.
> An it harm none, do what thou will.
> What we send forth will return thrice over, so we send it forth with light and love.
> So mote it be.

Visualize your prayers and wishes rising to the moon Goddess. Pick up the chalice or cup in your left hand and the athame or wand in your right hand and hold them at eye level then place the point of the athame or wand or your index finger into the wine and say:

> May male and female be joined and let all be fruitful throughout the land. The food I eat is the blessing of the Gods and I remember those who have none. I am grateful for all I have been given and am open and ready to receive that which is still to come.
> So mote it be.

> We have met in love and friendship, let us part the same way, spreading the love from this circle outward to all, sharing it with those we meet. Lord and Lady my thanks to you for sharing this time with me, guarding and guiding me.
> Merry we meet, merry we part, merry we meet again.
> The circle will now be closed.

Finish with:

> Take for your use, eastern watchtower, any powers of air that have not been used.
> Take for your use, southern watchtower, any powers of fire that have not been used.
> Take for your use, western watchtower, any powers of water that have not been used.

Take for your use, northern watchtower, any powers of earth that have not been used.

The circle is now closed but the work continues.

Let it harm none, so mote it be.

MABON FOODS

The foods associated with mabon include mushrooms, potatoes, grains, late summer/fall fruits and vegetables, especially corn, beans, and pumpkins, and soups of all kinds.

MABON RECIPES

POTATO SOUP

Serves 4

Potato is a great vehicle for soaking up the flavors from other foods. Be bold with the herbs you use and add plenty of salt and pepper. I sometimes add leftover chopped crispy bacon to my potato soup.

> 4 tablespoons (60 g) butter
> 3 large potatoes, thinly sliced
> 2 medium onions, thinly sliced
> 1 garlic clove, crushed
> 4¼ cups (1 liter) milk
> 1 sprig of thyme, whole
> 1 bay leaf
> 1 small bunch of parsley, whole
> Salt and freshly ground black pepper
> Chopped chives, to garnish

Melt the butter in a soup pot over low heat. Add the potatoes, onions, and garlic and toss well in the butter. Cover with a lid and sweat the vegetables for 10 minutes. Do not let them brown.

Add the milk, thyme, bay leaf, parsley, and a good pinch of salt and pepper, then simmer without boiling for 30 minutes. Remove the thyme, bay leaf, and parsley and set aside to cool.

Using a blender, food processor, or hand-held immersion blender, purée the soup for 1 minute (or until smooth, if you prefer). Return to the pot to heat through. Season with salt and pepper, if necessary. Pour into soup bowls and garnish with chopped chives.

LENTIL SOUP

2 tablespoons olive oil

2 large onions, finely chopped

3 garlic cloves, finely chopped

1 cup (200 g) yellow lentils

1 lb (450 g) carrots, grated

4¼ cups (1 liter) good-quality ham stock (page 25)

Salt and freshly ground black pepper

A splash of whole milk or cream, to serve

Warm the oil in a soup pot over low heat. Add the onions, garlic, and lentils and sweat until the onions change color, about 10 minutes, then add the carrots and stock and mix well.

Cover with a lid, increase the heat to high, bring to a boil, then reduce the heat to low and simmer for 1 hour, until the lentils are very soft. Taste and adjust the seasoning if needed, then set aside to cool.

Once the soup has cooled, usa a blender, food processor, or hand-held immersion blender to purée the soup until smooth, or to your desired consistency. Return to the pot to heat through. Serve hot, with a splash of milk or cream.

OLD-FASHIONED BROTH

Serves 6 to 8

1 whole leek

9 tablespoons (125 g) butter

A splash of olive oil

½ cup (100 g) dried soup mix (or mixed lentils, dried split peas,
and pearl barley)

6¼ cups (1.5 liters) good-qualiy ham stock (page 25)

2 potatoes, peeled and diced

6 large carrots, grated

½ turnip, peeled and diced

Salt and freshly ground black pepper

Crusty bread, to serve

Slice the green part of the leek into ¼-inch (6 mm) rings and place them in a colander under cold running water to clean them. Slice down the length of the white part to create two halves, then slice again so that you have four strips. Cut each strip into ¼-inch (6 mm) pieces, add to the colander with the green pieces, and run water over the pieces to clean them. Drain well.

Melt the butter and oil in a soup pot over low heat, then add the leeks and soup mix and sweat it until they start to change color, about 10 minutes. Add the ham stock and the vegetables, increase the heat to high, and bring to a boil. Cover the pot with a lid, reduce the heat to low, and simmer for 2–3 hours (the longer you cook it, the better it will taste). Season with salt and pepper to your liking. Serve with crusty bread to mop up all the broth.

MUSHROOM SOUP

Serves 4

8 oz (250 g) mushrooms

1 carrot, peeled and cut into chunks

1 white onion, peeled and cut into chunks

2½ cups (600 ml) stock (chicken or ham, pages 25–26)

2½ cups (600 ml) heavy whipping cream

Milk, if needed

Salt and freshly ground black pepper

Clean the mushrooms by wiping them with a dry cloth then put them in a soup pot over medium-high heat. Add the carrot, onion, and stock and bring to a boil. Reduce the heat to low and simmer until the carrot is soft, about 20 minutes. Remove from the heat and set aside to cool.

Using a blender, food processor, or hand-held immersion blender, purée the soup to a creamy consistency. Put the soup back in the pot, add the cream, and reheat over low heat; if your soup is too thick, use milk to thin it to your desired consistency. Taste and adjust the seasoning then serve.

LASAGNA

Serves 4 to 6

Lasagna is made of three elements: the bolognese sauce, the white sauce, and the pasta sheets. It takes time to put it all together, but it is so worth the effort. I always make mine in a large deep dish and when it is cool, I cut it into portions and freeze it for dinner on lazy days. Make the bolognese sauce first and let it cook while you prepare the rest.

> 1 portion Bolognese Sauce (page 202)
> 1 package lasagna sheets
> 1 tablespoon grated Parmesan cheese

> **White Sauce**
> Scant ½ cup (60 g) all-purpose flour
> 4 tablespoons (60 g) butter
> 1 oz (30 g) white cheddar cheese, grated
> 1 teaspoon grated nutmeg, plus extra to serve
> 2½ cups (600 ml) milk
> Salt and freshly ground black pepper

You can follow the traditional method to make the white sauce on page 31, adding nutmeg, salt, and pepper to flavor it.

Alteratively, here is a super-quick way to make the sauce. Put the flour, butter, cheddar cheese, nutmeg, and half of the milk into a blender or food processor and blend until smooth. Pour the contents into a nonstick saucepan over low heat, add the rest of the milk, and slowly bring to a boil, stirring continuously. Add salt and pepper to taste, and simmer for 5 minutes, or until thickened. Remove and set aside. You risk having an "uncooked flour" taste in the sauce if you make it this way; however, the lasagna is going to be baked in the oven so that taste is unlikely to remain by the time you serve it.

Putting It All Together

Preheat the oven to 350°F (180°C). Pour a little of the white sauce into a deep baking dish then lay enough pasta sheets to cover the bottom, breaking them to fit where necessary. Add half of the bolognese sauce, followed by half of the white sauce. Arrange another layer of pasta sheets on top, then add the rest of the bolognese. Place a final layer of pasta sheets on top, then cover with the rest of the white sauce. Grate some nutmeg over the top then sprinkle with the Parmesan. Bake for 40 minutes, until the pasta sheets are cooked and the top is browned.

ROASTED SWEET POTATOES

Serves 6 to 8

Sweet potatoes cook much quicker than ordinary potatoes no matter how you cook them. You can add chopped rosemary while roasting if you like.

>   4 medium sweet potatoes, washed, peeled, and quartered
>   1 tablespoon olive oil

Preheat the oven to 350°F (180°C). Place the sweet potatoes in a large bowl with the olive oil and mix with your hands until they are evenly coated with oil. Dump them onto a baking sheet. Bake for 50 minutes or until tender.

MAHSHI

Serves 6 to 8

Mahshi means "stuffed" in Arabic, and refers to a variety of stuffed vegetable dishes (the vine leaf version is called waraq enab). Be warned, this Middle Eastern recipe takes ages to make and does not even look very special but oh, the taste is simply divine! If you can make it last until the second day, you are a stronger person than me!

30 grape vine leaves or 4 spring cabbages
1 lb (450 g) ground beef or lamb (lamb is traditional)
Generous ¾ cups (250 g) basmati rice
4 tablespoons (60 g) butter
1 teaspoon each of salt and pepper, mixed
1 teaspoon dried mint, or 1 tablespoon fresh mint, chopped
1 garlic bulb, peeled and cloves separated
4 lemons, 1 juiced and 3 cut into wedges

If you are using vine leaves, chances are you will have purchased them in a package and they will be soft and pliable. If you are fortunate enough to obtain them fresh, follow the same blanching instructions as for the cabbage leaves to soften them. Leave vine leaves whole.

If you are using cabbage, cut the heavy stem from the bottom of each cabbage and one by one remove all the leaves. Half-fill a wide-bottom sauté pan with water, place over medium heat, and wait until the water comes to a boil. Take 3 or 4 cabbage leaves and put them in the pan of boiling water, just until the leaves become pliable, then remove them using tongs and set them aside to cool. Repeat this process until all the leaves have been blanched. Using a sharp knife, remove the center spine of each leaf so that you halve the leaves. Save the spines—you will use them later.

Place the beef in a bowl and, using your hands, break it up so that it is fairly loose and separated.

Place the rice in a jug, fill the jug with very hot water, stir a few times, then drain through a sieve. Repeat this process a few times until the water runs clear.

Add the rice to the beef while it is still warm from the water. Add the butter, salt, pepper, and mint, and carefully mix with your hands (if you can bear the heat); if it is too hot, use a spoon or spatula. Make sure the rice and beef are thoroughly blended together.

Lay all the cabbage spines and any broken vine leaves in the bottom of a large pot. Take one of the leaves (or half-leaves) and spoon a little of the rice and beef mixture (about a finger thick) along the bottom (diagonally if using cabbage). Roll up firmly, tucking in the ends as you go. Repeat, tightly layering the rolls on top of the cabbage spines in the pot. When one layer has been completed, throw in a couple of the garlic cloves, then start a new layer of rolled leaves, laying them in the opposite direction. Repeat this process until you run out of leaves or rice and beef mixture. If you have any leftover rice and beef mixture, you can stuff it into bell peppers, zucchinis, or even tomatoes. If you have leftover leaves, you can lay them across the top of your finished rolled leaves and just eat them at the end.

Once you have finished your layers, weigh them down with an upturned (heatsafe) plate placed inside the pot. Pour in cold water until it reaches the top of the rolls in the pot. Set over medium-high heat and bring to a boil, then reduce the heat to low and simmer for 4 hours. If the pot starts to run out of water before the filling is cooked, just add another cup of water as needed and continue to cook.

To serve, pile the mahshi neatly on a large oval platter. Sprinkle with lemon juice, then garnish with the lemon wedges. Serve hot or at room temperature.

CABBAGE RICE

Serves 4

This is a lazy version of Mahshi (page 230) that has the same flavors (though a different look) and is made in much less time.

1 head of cabbage, shredded
3 lemons, halved

Perfect Rice
1 cup (200 g) basmati rice
2 cups (480 ml) water or stock
Boiling water, for soaking
1 or 2 cloves (optional)

Start the rice: Bring the measured water or stock to a boil in a stockpot and set aside. Put the rice into a large heatproof jug and cover with boiling water. Leave the rice to soak in the water for 5 minutes, stirring it once or twice. You will see the starch rising to the surface.

Drain the rice in a sieve, add it to the pot with the boiling liquid, then add the shredded cabbage on top. Bring the pot to a boil, reduce the heat to its lowest setting, and cover with a tight-fitting lid. Do not stir and do not touch for at least 10 minutes. One or two cloves added to basmati rice while it is cooking will help to ward off negative influences as well as tasting good!

After the 10 minutes, lift the lid and check the rice—there should be small air holes all over the surface. Replace the lid, turn off the heat, and leave the pot to stand for another 10 minutes, cooking in its own heat. It will then be ready to serve. If you added cloves, you can remove them before serving.

To serve, fill a bowl with the cabbage and rice and serve with lemon halves for squeezing.

BAKED MACKEREL

Serves 2

Where I live, fresh mackerel is difficult to get unless you know someone who goes fishing and has plenty to spare, so when I do get some I fillet it and prepare it for cooking, then freeze it. When I want to cook it, I remove it from the freezer and put it straight into the oven. Your fishmonger can fillet the mackerel for you.

4 mackerel fillets
8 tablespoons (115 g) butter, diced
Lemon wedges, to serve
Crusty bread, to serve (optional)

For the Marinade
2 tablespoons lemon juice
12 whole black peppercorns, crushed
8 whole green peppercorns, crushed
6–8 sprigs of fresh rosemary (adjust to suit your taste), bruised

Preheat the oven to 425°F (220°C). Make the marinade: In a bowl, combine the lemon juice, crushed peppercorns, and rosemary and mix well.

Lay each fish fillet skin side up on a chopping board and, using a sharp knife, make 3 diagonal cuts into the flesh. Dot some of the butter into each cut. Pour marinade over the top of each fish. Wrap in foil, place on a baking sheet, and bake for 15 minutes until the fish is cooked.

Delicious served with lemon wedges and crusty bread.

NOTE: If you want to freeze the fish, put the marinated fillets in a freezer-safe container and put it straight into the freezer. When you are ready to cook the fish, extend the cooking time by 6 minutes.

MUSHROOMS

Wild mushrooms are in season from around late August to December, but of course they are available in shops all year round. Still, it is nice to give a nod to this season by celebrating Mabon with a few mushroom dishes.

Never pick wild mushrooms unless you know exactly what you are doing because some types are deadly poisonous. The rule, as always, with foraged food is "if in doubt—do not eat."

Mushrooms should never be washed because they tend to get slimy if they are cleaned with water. If they need to be cleaned, wipe them with a clean kitchen towel or paper towel. Mushrooms are quick and easy to prepare, and the following pages have a few of my favorite recipes.

BREAKFAST MUSHROOMS *Serves 1*

This is also nice dish for Samhain breakfast if served with Cinnamon Pancakes (see the variation on page 36).

> A splash of olive oil
> 4 tablespoons (60 g) butter
> 6 black peppercorns, roughly crushed
> 4 fresh chestnut or cremini mushrooms, cleaned and quartered
> 6 pink peppercorns, roughly crushed
> Juice of ½ lemon

Warm the oil in a frying pan over low heat, then add the butter. Once the butter has melted, add the peppercorns and stir a couple of times. Increase the heat to high and add the mushrooms. Let them sit for 5 minutes, then stir them with a spoon or spatula or give the pan a couple of good shakes, so that the mushrooms are browned all over. Just before serving, drizzle with the lemon juice.

MUSHROOMS WITH GARLIC AND PINK PEPPERCORNS

Serves 4

1 teaspoon olive oil

1 garlic clove, finely chopped

2 tablespoons (30 g) butter

6 oz (180 g) fresh mushrooms (any variety), cleaned and
halved or sliced

10 pink peppercorns

Warm the oil and garlic in a frying pan over low heat then add the butter. Once the butter has melted, increase the heat to high and toss in the mushrooms and the pink peppercorns. Keep the mushrooms moving around in the hot pan for about 5 minutes, making sure they are well covered with the oil and butter. Serve immediately.

MUSHROOMS WITH CHEESE SAUCE

Serves 4

1 tablespoon olive oil

6 oz (180 g) fresh mushrooms (any variety), cleaned and
halved or sliced

½ cup (125 ml) heavy cream

Scant 2 cups (125 g) grated cheese (your preference)

Crusty bread, to serve

Warm the oil in a frying pan over high heat then add the mushrooms and cook for 5 minutes.

Warm the cream in a saucepan over low heat and add the grated cheese. Stir until the cheese has melted, then add the mushrooms. Stir until the mushrooms are warm and coated evenly in the cheese sauce. Serve immediately with crusty bread.

NOTE: Various herbs can be added to the cheese sauce to suit your celebration or ritual work.

STUFFED MUSHROOMS

Serves 6

6 large white, chestnut, or cremini mushrooms, cleaned, stalks
removed and reserved
1 tablespoon olive oil
1 small onion, finely chopped
1 tablespoon fresh breadcrumbs
1 tablespoon heavy cream
Freshly grated cheese (optional)
A handful of freshly chopped herbs that suit your magickal or
ritual work (optional)

Preheat the oven to 425°F (220°C). Set the mushroom heads upside down on a baking sheet and set the stalks aside.

Warm the oil in a frying pan over medium-low heat and gently fry the onion until it is translucent. Meanwhile, finely dice the mushroom stalks and when the onions are translucent, add the stalks to the pan. Continue to cook slowly until the stalks have softened, about 5 minutes.

Add the breadcrumbs and stir in the heavy cream, a tablespoon at a time, until you have a thick mixture that can be easily spooned into the mushroom heads.

Add heaped spoonfuls of the stuffing mixture into the upturned mushroom heads. You can sprinkle over grated cheese or herbs before baking, but they are also delicious without. Bake the mushrooms for 20–30 minutes, until the tops are golden.

STUFFED ZUCCHINIS

Serves 1

1 small onion, finely chopped

2 garlic cloves, finely chopped

1 tablespoon olive oil, plus extra for drizzling

4 tablespoons (60 g) butter

1 mushroom, finely diced

1 zucchini, rinsed and halved lengthways (do not cut off
    the tops and bottoms)

Freshly grated cheese, to garnish (optional)

A handful of freshly chopped herbs that suit your magickal or
    ritual work (optional), to garnish

Preheat the oven to 350°F (180°C). Put the onion and garlic in a frying pan over low heat with the olive oil and butter. Cook slowly without browning the onions, for about 5 minutes, then add the mushrooms.

Drag a teaspoon along the inside of the zucchinis to scoop out the soft center. Dice the soft insides, add them to the pan, and cook for a few minutes.

Place the zucchini shells on a baking sheet, skin side down and fill with the mushroom mixture, then drizzle with a little olive oil. Bake for 20–30 minutes, until the zucchinis are tender. You can sprinkle grated cheese over the tops and/or sprinkle with fresh herbs to suit your spell or ritual work.

RICE AND GREEN LENTILS

Serves 4 to 6

The recipe for this fantastic dish is made up of three stages. In part one, you prepare the rice and green lentils. In part two, onions and garlic are caramelized. In part three, the tomato salad traditionally served with this dish is prepared. Put them all together and the result is wonderful!

Part One

½ cup (90 g) green lentils

1 cup (200 g) basmati rice

2 cups (480 ml) water or stock

Boiling water, for soaking

1 or 2 cloves (optional)

Part Two

3 large onions, finely sliced

3 garlic cloves, crushed or chopped

2 teaspoons sugar

1 tablespoon olive oil

Part Three, Tomato Salad

2 onions, finely chopped

6 fresh tomatoes, cut into chunks

1 garlic clove, crushed

1 sprig fresh or 1 teaspoon dried basil

1 sprig fresh or 1 teaspoon dried oregano

1 sprig fresh or 1 teaspoon dried mint

1 tablespoon olive oil

1 fresh lemon, halved

Salt and freshly ground black pepper

Part One

Put the green lentils into a small pot and half-fill it with water. Bring to a boil and simmer until they begin to swell around the edges, but are not cooked through, about 5 minutes. Drain.

Meanwhile, start the rice: Bring the measured water or stock to a boil in a stockpot and set aside.

Put the rice into a large heatproof jug and cover with boiling water. Leave the rice to soak in the water for 5 minutes, stirring it once or twice. You will see the starch rising to the surface.

Drain the rice in a sieve, add it to the stockpot with the boiling liquid, then add the parboiled lentils and the cloves, if using. Bring to a boil, reduce the heat to its lowest setting, and cover with a tight-fitting lid. Do not stir and do not touch for at least 10 minutes.

After the 10 minutes, lift the lid and check the rice—there should be small air holes all over the surface. Replace the lid, turn off the heat, and leave the pot to stand for another 10 minutes, cooking in its own heat.

Part Two
In a frying pan, combine the onions, garlic, sugar, and cook over low heat for 10 minutes, stirring often, until caramelized; the sugar will help to brown and caramelize them, but if you cook this too fast and do not stir it enough it will burn and ruin the dish. Keep your eye on it. While this magick is happening, you can make the tomato salad.

Part Three
Put the onions and tomatoes in a deep salad bowl and add the garlic and herbs. Add the olive oil and stir well. Squeeze one lemon half over the salad, stir, and taste, adding more lemon juice and salt and pepper until you achieve the taste you like. Put this aside.

Putting It All Together
When the rice and green lentils are cooked, remove the cloves, if using, and mix in the fried onion mixture, stirring once or twice. Serve on a nice plate garnished with the tomato salad and some crusty bread on the side to soak up the juice from the salad.

SCOTCH PANCAKES

Serves 3

I find the best way to mix this pancake batter is to use a clear glass measuring jug, but the choice is yours—you can just use a mixing bowl if you prefer.

> 1⅔ cups (180 g) self-rising flour
> ½ teaspoon baking powder
> Scant ½ cup (90 g) sugar
> 1 teaspoon maple syrup
> 1 egg
> ⅔ cups (150 ml) milk
> Sunflower oil, for frying

Place the flour, baking powder, and sugar into a jug (or bowl) and stir a few times. Add the syrup (which gives the pancakes a nice golden color), egg, and about half of the milk, and stir. The mixture at this stage will be cloggy with lots of loose flour. Add the rest of the milk and stir again—there should be no loose flour and the mixture should be fairly thick.

Beat the mixture using a fork or whisk. The mixture has the right consistency when it drops heavily and slowly from your fork or whisk. For best results, place the batter in the refrigerator for 10 minutes and leave it to "work its own magick."

Heat a few drops of sunflower oil in a nonstick pan (that's the secret of a good pancake) and place over medium heat. Use a paper towel or silicone brush to rub the oil around the base and sides of the pan. Take the pancake batter out of the refrigerator and stir it—it may have thickened but don't adjust it yet. Using a tablespoon with a pointed end, drop a heaped spoonful at a time into the hot pan. As soon as bubbles appear on the surface, use a spatula or pallet knife to flip the pancake over. As soon as you flip it, push down on the pancake gently. This process should take 1–2 minutes in total. If the pancake is too pale, raise the heat a little; if it is too brown, lower the heat. If it looks too thick, add a teaspoon more milk to the batter and stir well. I usually cook four small pancakes at a time in the pan, after gauging the first for consistency and degree of heat. Keep the cooked pancakes in a folded tea towel on a cooling rack until ready to eat.

VARIATION: Apples make a delicious addition to Scotch Pancakes. Peel and dice or grate 1 apple and add it to the pancake batter before cooking. Serve hot, drizzled with cream, or eat cold.

DANISH APPLE CRUMBLE

Serves 4

Crumble

2⅔ cups (315 g) all-purpose flour

A pinch of salt

Scant 1 cup (180 g) sugar

14 tablespoons (210 g) butter

Filling

1 oz (30 g) dried mixed fruit

1 lb (450 g) apples, coarsely chopped

⅓ cup (60 g) sugar

A pinch of ground cinnamon

Butter, for greasing

Whipped cream or Custard (page 32), to serve

Preheat the oven to 350°F (180°C) and generously grease an 8-inch (20 cm) baking dish with butter.

Make the crumble topping: In a large bowl, combine the flour, salt, and sugar and mix well. Add the butter and rub it into the flour mixture with your fingers until it resembles fine breadcrumbs.

Next, make the filling: In a bowl, mix the dried fruit and the chopped apples together, sprinkle with the sugar and cinnamon, and stir well.

Place the fruit into a well-greased 8-inch (20 cm) baking dish then sprinkle the crumble mixture on top. Bake for 40–45 minutes, until the crumble is browned and the fruit mixture is bubbling.

Serve with whipped cream or custard.

VARIATION: You could also make this crumble with a stewed rhubarb filling instead of apple. In a medium saucepan, combine 10 thin red sticks of rhubarb (choppped), ½–⅔ cup (100–130 g) sugar (to taste), and 2 tablespoons of water over medium-low heat. Simmer, stirring occasionally, until the sugar has dissolved and the rhubarb is soft, about 15 minutes.

LADIES' FINGERS

Serves 4

6 oz (180 g) okra, tops and bottoms removed, cut into
  1-inch (2.5 cm) pieces

1 tablespoon olive oil

1 large onion, finely chopped

2 garlic cloves, crushed

14 oz (400 g) can chopped tomatoes, or 1 lb (450 g)
  fresh tomatoes, chopped

10.75 oz (305 g) can tomato paste, or to taste

Water, stock, plain yogurt, or buttermilk, as needed

Perfect Rice, to serve (page 35, made from 1 cup/200 g rice)

Soak the okra in a bowl of water for 15 minutes to wash away the slimy juices.

Warm the oil in a sauté pan (use one that has a lid) over medium-low heat, then fry the onion and garlic slowly until the onion is translucent. Drain the okra, add it to the pan, and cook for 10 minutes. Add the tomatoes, cook for a further 10 minutes, then add the tomato paste to taste.

Cover the pan with a lid and simmer very gently over low heat for 20 minutes. Check the thickness of the mixture frequently and add a little water or stock or a dollop of plain yogurt or buttermilk as needed to prevent it from sticking or becoming too thick.

Serve on top of the Perfect Rice.

APPLE JELLY

Makes 4–5 cups (1.1–1.3 kg)

2 lb (900 g) Granny Smith or other tart green apples, rinsed
    in cold water and quartered
Sugar (1 lb/500 g of sugar to 2¼ cups/500 ml of liquid)
A pat of butter (omit if processing for longer-term storage)

Put the apples in a large pot and add enough water to just cover them. Bring to a boil then reduce the heat to low and simmer for 30 minutes, then set aside to cool.

Find somewhere to hang your jelly bag (an upturned kitchen chair works well) and place a clean pot underneath. Take your pot of cooled fruit and carefully pour the contents into the jelly bag then leave the liquid to slowly drip through the bag overnight. Do not be tempted to force the liquid through the bag or your jelly could become cloudy.

The next day, wash some jam jars in hot soapy water then sterilize them (see page 57).

Measure the amount of apple liquid you have strained to figure out the correct ratio of sugar: You will need 1 lb (500 g) of sugar for every 2¼ cups (500 ml) of liquid.

Put your liquid and the sugar into a large pot and place over low heat until the sugar has dissolved—do not leave the pot alone because it could boil over. Then increase the heat and bring to a rolling boil until set. As it gets near its setting point (after about 20 minutes), the liquid begins to rise up in the pot to twice or three times its volume and it begins to develop a foam on the top—you can add the butter to remove the foam, or skim it off with a slotted spoon (do not use butter if processing for longer-term storage).

To test that it is set, place a teaspoon of the jelly on a chilled saucer. Let it sit for a few minutes then draw your finger across the jelly on the saucer. If it leaves a wrinkle and the jelly doesn't flow back together again then it is set. If it has not set, continue to boil for another few minutes and repeat. At setting point, turn off the heat and ladle the jelly into your hot jars.

Allow to cool and then cover and store in the refrigerator for up to 1 month. Alternatively, process for longer term pantry storage according to the instructions on page 171.

DAMSON JELLY

Makes 4–5 cups (1.1–1.3 kg)

2 lb (900 g) damsons
1 lb (450 g) cooking apples, rinsed in cold water and quartered
Sugar (2 lb/900 g sugar for each 1¼ cups/1 liter juice)
A pat of butter (omit if processing for longer-term storage)

Put all the fruit in a large pot, add enough water to just cover the fruit, and place over low heat. Simmer slowly until the fruit is tender, then coarsely mash. Set aside to cool a little.

Find somewhere to hang your jelly bag (an upturned kitchen chair works well) and place a clean pot underneath. Carefully pour the cooled contents of your pot into the jelly bag, then leave the liquid to slowly drip through the bag overnight. Do not be tempted to force the liquid through the jelly bag or your jelly could become cloudy.

The next day, wash some jam jars in hot soapy water then sterilize them (see page 57).

Measure the amount of juice you have strained to figure out the correct ratio of sugar: You will need 1 lb (500 g) of sugar for every 2¼ cups (500 ml) of liquid. Put your liquid and the sugar into a large pot and place over low heat until the sugar has dissolved—do not leave the pot alone because it could boil over. Then increase the heat and bring to a rolling boil until set. As it gets near its setting point (after about 20 minutes), the liquid begins to rise up in the pot to twice or three times its volume and it begins to develop a foam on the top—you can add the butter to remove the foam, or skim it off with a slotted spoon (do not use butter if processing for longer-term storage).

To test that it is set, place a teaspoon of the jelly on a chilled saucer. Let it sit for a few minutes then draw your finger across the jelly on the saucer. If it leaves a wrinkle and the jelly doesn't flow back together again then it is set. If it has not set, continue to boil for another few minutes then do another test. At setting point, turn off the heat and ladle the jelly into your hot jars.

Allow to cool and then cover and store in the refrigerator for up to 1 month. Alternatively, process for longer term pantry storage according to the instructions on page 171.

KITCHEN WITCH REMEDIES

CLEANING THE WITCH WAY

Your cleaning cupboards could be filled with a multitude of harmful and dangerous chemicals. I don't know about you, but I hate the thought of pouring these potentially harmful chemicals down the drain and into the environment.

The good news is you don't always have to use strong chemicals. Here are a few suggestions for some natural cleaners that you will enjoy all the more because:

a)   they are not harmful to you or the environment

b)   you have made them yourself

c)   they work really well

d)   they smell good

e)   they cost less than branded cleaning products (buy ingredients in bulk if you can).

If you have fancy nonstick coatings on your pots and pans or delicate fabrics that need to be specially cleaned, you must first consult the manufacturer's instructions before using any products. Even natural substances can be strongly damaging to certain delicate substances. For example, if you have marble surfaces, even natural fruit acids could damage them (you should see what pineapple juice did to my marble pastry slab).

Your basic cupboard should contain some items that you can mix according to what you wish to clean. The following are essential.

BAKING SODA

Essential for lots of baked items, baking soda is also a great cleaning product, but do not use it on aluminum products.

Mix it with a little water to make a paste—great for cleaning tea and coffee stains from china. Run out of fabric softener? Use a spoonful of baking soda in your rinse cycle.

To clean silver, place a piece of crumpled aluminum foil in a basin of boiling water, place the silver on top, and sprinkle on some baking soda. There will then be a chemical reaction that removes the tarnish from the silver. Then simply rinse the silver items in water, dry, and buff with a soft cloth.

WHITE VINEGAR

Great for cutting through grease and leaving shiny surfaces squeaky clean. Pour it onto crumpled newspapers and rub on your windows to make them streak free.

If you have a puppy or kitten that has urinated on your carpet, a diluted vinegar solution will help clean and deodorize the area.

Spray weeds with neat vinegar instead of harmful weedkillers.

SALT

Useful in combination with vinegar and lemon as an abrasive to get stubbornly dirty or greasy surfaces clean.

Salt is a natural deodorizer—see the next page for a recipe for carpet freshener made from salt.

A paste of salt water and cream of tartar will remove rust stains from metal.

LEMONS

A lemon half—squeezed dry from another recipe—can be turned into a pot scourer with a little salt. The scent is attractive and the acid aids in cleaning. Add lemon juice to your vinegar-based cleaning mixtures to improve the smell.

ESSENTIAL OILS

I buy melt-and-pour glycerin soap, paraben-free shampoos and conditioners, and bath oils and I add a variety of essential oils to them to suit my mood or occasion. Essential oils can be used to perfume, deodorize, disinfect, and stimulate, as well as to repel house pests without harming them. Use them as room sprays, in oil burners, in baths, and during a massage.

RECIPES FOR CLEANING PRODUCTS

WOOD FURNITURE CLEANER

½ cup (60 ml) olive oil
½ cup (60 ml) freshly
squeezed lemon juice
1 teaspoon (5 ml) lemon
essential oil

Mix in a bottle, label, and shake well before each application. To use, place a few drops on a soft, clean cloth and rub over the wood then rub again with a clean cloth.

CARPET FRESHENER

Table salt
1 teaspoon each lavender,
geranium, and lemon
essential oil (or your
favorites)

Fill a 1-quart (1-liter) container three-quarters of the way to the top with table salt then add the oils. You can vary these oils to suit your preference, but for this purpose they are my favorites. Give the container a good shake, and label it. When you are ready to use it, sprinkle it liberally over all your carpets and leave it for about ten minutes, then vacuum as normal. Your carpets will smell fresh and clean.

SPRAY, ALL-PURPOSE CLEANER (BATHROOMS)

2½ cups (600 ml) water
1 teaspoon baking soda
10 drops pine essential oil
10 drops lemon essential oil
5 drops thyme essential oil

Add all the ingredients to a spray bottle then label. Shake well before each use, spray on your surface, and wipe off immediately with a clean cloth. Do not spray and leave on wooden surfaces because this will leave spots of dried baking soda. If this happens, it is easily resolved—just spray again and rub off.

SPRAY, ALL-PURPOSE CLEANER (KITCHENS)

2½ cups (600 ml) water
1 teaspoon baking soda
20 drops lemon essential oil

Add all ingredients to a spray bottle then label and shake well before using. This cleaner will not only clean but also disinfect, and it is not harmful so you can use it anywhere in your kitchen, including your food storage cabinets/pantry, and refrigerator.

AIR FRESHENER
(SPRING OR SUMMER BLEND)

> 2½ cups (600 ml) water
> 10 drops lemon, lavender,
>   or geranium essential oil
>   (or a combination)

Add the ingredients to a spray bottle, label, and shake well before each use. The freshener can be sprayed onto carpets, but avoid spraying directly onto curtains made from delicate fabrics.

AIR FRESHENER
(AUTUMN OR WINTER BLEND)

> 2½ cups (600 ml) water
> 10 drops orange, nutmeg, or
>   frankincense essential
>   oil (or a combination)

Add the ingredients to a spray bottle, label, and shake well before each use. This can be sprayed onto carpets, but avoid spraying directly onto curtains made from delicate fabrics.

AIR FRESHENER
(BEDROOM BLEND)

> 2½ cups (600 ml) water
> 10 drops sandalwood,
>   patchouli, or geranium
>   essential oil (or a
>   combination)

Add the ingredients to a spray bottle, label, and shake well before each use. This can be sprayed onto carpets, but avoid spraying directly onto curtains made from delicate fabrics.

AIR FRESHENER
(BATHROOM BLEND)

> 2½ cups (600 ml) water
> 10 drops pine or lemon
>   essential oil (or a
>   combination)
> A few drops thyme essential oil

Add the ingredients to a spray bottle, label, and shake well before each use. This can be sprayed onto carpets, but avoid spraying directly onto curtains made from delicate fabrics.

LOTIONS AND POTIONS

Please do not assume that these replace medical treatment. They do not. If you are unwell, you should be seen by a doctor—let's not beat about the bush here. Do not try and diagnose yourself from the pages of a book or from the internet. But minor ailments, such as coughs, colds, spots, aches, and bruises, can sometimes be soothed with remedies from your pantry. If symptoms persist, you need to see the doctor though, no arguments!

A REMEDY FOR ATHLETE'S FOOT

The simplest way to treat athlete's foot is to put one drop of the following oil blend on a cotton ball and apply it to the infected area.

> 1 teaspoon base oil
> (such as almond)
> 1 drop frankincense oil
> 1 drop thyme oil
> 1 drop lemon oil

Label and store in an essential oil bottle and dab onto the affected areas as needed.

NOTE: Tea tree oil is a great oil with antibacterial and antifungal properties and is also worth a try for athlete's foot.

A POULTICE

This is a very old remedy. The warmth of a poultice can bring a spot, boil, or abscess to a head or ease pain from sprains and aches. It is also said to help draw out splinters.

BREAD POULTICE

Break some bread into small pieces and moisten with milk then place on the infected area and cover with a light bandage. Remove every morning and make a new poultice until the infection has cleared. If there is no marked difference after two days, seek medical advice from your pharmacist or doctor.

SOAP POULTICE

Grate a bar of laundry or kitchen soap, add a little sugar, moisten, and place over an infected area and wrap in a clean bandage. Change daily, but if symptoms persist and the infection is not cleared after two days, consult your pharmacist or doctor.

FOR COLDS

You cannot cure a cold. There is also not much you can do to avoid catching one—though regular hand washing helps. However, you can soothe your symptoms by doing a few things.

CONGESTION

Alleviate the horrid nasal congestion of a cold with this remedy.

> 1 drop eucalyptus oil
> 1 drop peppermint oil
> 1 drop tea tree oil
> Boiling water

Place the essential oils in a bowl of boiling water. Put a towel over your head and inhale the vapors from the bowl for 5 minutes, keeping your eyes closed.

DRINK...

- Plenty of water and juice, but avoid caffeinated drinks.
- Chicken soup—no medical evidence whatsoever that it helps, but it certainly will not do any harm! It is very nutritious, delicious, and soothing, so why not?
- A mug of boiling water or lemonade with 1 teaspoon freshly grated ginger, juice of ½ lemon, and 1 teaspoon honey. Sip while you are wrapped up in bed!

COUGH SYRUP

Slice an onion or some garlic and place in a bowl, layering it with sugar or honey (honey is a cough suppressant). Cover and leave overnight. Pour off the resulting syrup into a bottle, label, and store in the refrigerator until required. When needed, take a teaspoonful and stay warm. Try to avoid dramatic temperature changes because this will make you cough more.

SORE THROAT

Pot Marigold Syrup (page 251) is excellent for treating a sore throat. Take one teaspoonful three times a day. Hold it in your mouth for a moment and let it slowly trickle down your throat.

A tea made with cardamom and cinnamon also effectively cures a sore throat and hoarseness during the onset of a flu. Gargle daily as a protection from the flu.

A HEAD-CLEARING AROMATHERAPY BLEND

Use the following blend when you feel choked up with a cold or flu. Just add it to a warm bath and have a good soak.

> 3 drops rosemary
>   essential oil
> 3 drops tea tree essential oil
> 3 drops eucalyptus
>   essential oil

POT MARIGOLD SYRUP— GRANNY'S MAGICK SYRUP

Be sure to use the old-fashioned *Calendula officinalis* variety, also known as pot marigold. Calendula is antiseptic, anti-fungal, antidepressant, anti-inflammatory, and it also strengthens the immune system. For women, it is especially helpful during menstruation or menopause and, as if that was not enough, it can be made into a cream and applied to cuts and grazes to aid the healing process. My granddaughter Ashi calls this syrup I make from it "Granny's Magick Syrup." I always keep a jar in the refrigerator for anyone who complains of a sore throat or a cold.

> 4 loosely-packed cups
>   marigold petals
>   (*Calendula officinalis*)
> Boiling water
> Brown or white sugar
>   (your preference)
> 2 drops pure calendula
>   essential oil (you can
>   also use lavender)

Fill a 1-quart (1 liter) pot with petals, place over low heat, and add boiling water to reach almost to the top of the pan. Simmer until the volume has reduced by about 2 inches (5 cm). Remove from the heat and set aside to cool. When the mixture has cooled, strain the liquid through cheesecloth until all the juices are extracted, 1–2 hours.

Measure the remaining marigold liquid in a measuring cup. Put the liquid back into the pan over high heat and for each 1 cup (240 ml) of liquid, add the equivalent amount of sugar. Bring to a boil then reduce the heat to low and simmer until the mixture has reduced by about 2 inches (5 cm). Remove the mixture from the heat, add the pure calendula essential oil, and leave to cool. (I have used lavender before and it is also really lovely.) When the mixture is cool, pour into jars and store in the refrigerator.

CALENDULA CREAM

Mix some plain unperfumed moisturizer with drops of pure calendula essential oil for a great healing cream.

HEADACHE REMEDY

If you are having headaches regularly, you need to see a doctor. But if your headache is mild and you don't want to pop a pill, you can make a tea from a few smashed cardamom pods infused in boiling water to help relieve it. Teas made from lemon, marjoram, and rosemary are also said to help soothe headaches.

REMEDIES FOR COLD SORES

Cold sores (fever blisters) happen when you are run down and not looking after yourself, so try to avoid letting that happen in the first place! Drink plenty of water, eat fruits and vegetables, avoid stress, and get enough of vitamins A, C, and E, zinc, and iron. Lysine supplements are also recommended.

Regularly drinking an infusion made from the herb lemon balm is said to help prevent cold sores. Throw away your toothbrush after an attack and replace it regularly as a rule. Avoid sun and wind exposure.

If attacks are regular, consider cutting out chocolate, processed cereals, sodas, peas, peanuts, almonds, animal gelatin, and beer from your diet. Add a little more red meat, milk, eggs, cheese, real licorice, and fish to your diet.

There is no cure for cold sores, but a few natural remedies can soothe them and reduce the time they appear. Avoid other harsh-sounding remedies that might inflame your skin—they might work for some people, but you risk a nasty adverse reaction.

Witch hazel can help dry up a cold sore.

Sooth by applying cold milk using a cotton ball.

Collect the rosehips from wild rose bushes and make a tea. Crush the rosehips slightly and infuse in boiled water. Drink it sweetened with manuka honey or dab it, cooled, straight onto the cold sore.

You can also apply some pure calendula oil or some healing calendula cream from the recipe on page 251.

If the sore looks infected, tea tree oil has antibacterial and antiviral qualities and can be dabbed straight onto the skin with a cotton ball.

INDIGESTION REMEDY

Roughly grind some cardamom, ginger, cloves, and coriander seeds and infuse in boiling water to make a tea as a remedy for indigestion.

A REMEDY FOR BAD BREATH

Chew a few cardamom seeds for a few minutes.

REMEDIES FOR "THE BLUES"

If you have depression, you should see your doctor or mental health professional, but the temporary day-to-day blues, the kind where you can pinpoint a cause for your sadness, you can treat with a few soothing remedies.

Cardamom tea helps to soothe sadness, as does my Pot Marigold Syrup (page 251). Take one teaspoon of marigold syrup to lift your spirits when feeling down, but if you really have the blues take it three times a day.

INDEX

SORAYA

Soraya is a numerologist, astrologer, white witch, psychic, and internationally renowned author. She is author of The Mystery of the Wooden Rose Series of paranormal romantic mystery novels, *Tarot*, *Book of Spells*, *Enhance Your Psychic Powers*, *Runes*, *The Witch's Companion*, *The Little Book of Spells*, and *The Little Book of Cord and Candle Magick*.